SEX IN THE BRAIN

SEX IN THE BRAIN

A Neuropsychosexual Approach to Love and Intimacy

Janice Hiller

KARNAC
firing the mind

First published in 2024 by
Karnac Books Limited
62 Bucknell Road
Bicester
Oxfordshire OX26 2DS

British Library Cataloguing in Publication Data

A C.I.P. for this book is available from the British Library

ISBN: 978-1-91349-488-9 (paperback)
ISBN: 978-1-91349-489-6 (e-book)

Typeset by vPrompt eServices Pvt Ltd, India

Printed in the United Kingdom

www.firingthemind.com

For my family and friends

Living brains, along with their minds—the invisible manifestation of their network level neurobiological functions—reflect a delicate balance, as yet poorly understood, among vastly interacting neural circuits that work in and for living bodies and that respond to the challenges of the world by creating desired circumstances and avoiding those that are harmful. Emotional feelings are the experienced affective manifestations of such interactions; they are the subjective qualities of mind.

(Panksepp & Bevan, 2012, p. 500)

We now know that mind, brain and body are indivisible and that disorders traditionally thought of as psychological need to be reconceptualised to include their neurobiological and somatic component ... psychotherapy increases neural integration through challenges that expand our experience of and perspective on ourselves and the world. The challenge of expanding consciousness is to move beyond reflex, fear and prejudice to a mindfulness and compassion for ourselves and others. Understanding the promise and limitations of our brains is but one essential step in the evolution of human consciousness.

(Cozolino, 2017, p. 417)

Contents

Preface and acknowledgements

When I began putting together my ideas on how neuroscience could inform psychosexual therapy I thought there might be enough for a journal article. Then, as I researched deeper into the literature, I found the sheer range of the topic had increased considerably, and the project took off. I had to face the possibility of the article becoming a book, which was at the same time an exciting but daunting prospect. Neurobiology, romantic relationships, and sexual desire are topics I have presented frequently at lectures and workshops for Confer Events, the College of Sexual and Relationship Therapy, and at Tavistock Relationships during the time I was there as academic tutor in psychosexual studies. I have also published papers in peer-reviewed journals on the subject. As I read more I could see how these fascinating areas of neuroscience can offer real insights into how our mind–brain connections enable us to become unique individuals, with a personal identity based on environmental experiences, and with ever-evolving neural networks that will inform our life decisions and our intimate relationships.

People sometimes ask how neuroscience can be useful for clinical work that is really all about emotions and behaviour. My reply is that research into neuroscience can complement therapeutic methods by giving us another lens through which to view the human condition. I try to explain that neuroscience also demonstrates how we are all embedded in a social and cultural context that has shaped, and continues to shape, our neural circuitry over the lifespan, making it possible to self-reflect, adapt our behaviour, and relate to others. In the public domain there has been a growing awareness and interest in the role of neurotransmitters and brain structures. References to the amygdala, dopamine, and oxytocin are made quite often in the media these days, suggesting that people are curious about how the mind, brain, and the body interact. And when it comes to relationships and sexual desires, many of us would like to know more about the impacts of brain phenomena on our behaviour. My hope is that this book will add to that understanding.

Although I am not a trained neuroscientist, I have been studying the role of neurobiology pertaining to sexual behaviour for more than twenty years. Nevertheless, there may be errors in this book due to the complexity of the subject, the amount of research to cover, and despite my careful reading and cross-checking. This is a very challenging area with many ambiguities, as with most areas in science. I have attempted to understand the issues and give an account of how they may be applied to our sex lives and to psychosexual therapy; and if there are mistakes, they will be due to my struggles with the density of the empirical research. Also, considerable simplification has taken place in the diagrams because I wanted them to convey a visual image of a hugely intricate set of brain pathways and neurotransmitters. Notwithstanding the complexities, I am convinced that learning more about how neural connections underpin all our emotions and behaviours is a worthwhile endeavour and is one that can only deepen our understanding of how we engage with each other and the world.

This book might not have come about without the encouragement of Christina Wipf Perry formerly at Confer/Karnac, who fortunately attended a Confer talk I gave in early 2020. Christina was very positive about providing assistance as I developed the article I was writing into a book. Her confidence that this could happen made a big difference, and I am most grateful for her support. Others at Karnac Books have been helpful as the work progressed. Especial thanks are due to Brigid Hekster who has carefully and generously read and commented on every chapter, providing insightful ideas and suggestions that have undoubtedly improved the text enormously. I am very grateful to Brigid for her input. Karen Rogers kindly worked on checking the references, which is much appreciated. I would also like to thank Julia Margo, Sonia Sodha, and Stephanie Cohen, who have been enthusiastic about my project, each in their own way, and helped it to be fun. Thanks are definitely due to Steve Salkind, whose analytic approach to complicated research results has aided my understanding. Steve's assistance and technical skills in designing the diagrams with me has been invaluable, and his patience with my focus on getting the book done has given me the space and energy to complete the task.

About the author

Janice Hiller is a consultant clinical psychologist who worked in the NHS in adult mental health initially, before specialising in sexology. She set up and ran the Relationship and Psychosexual Service in North-East London, and then joined Tavistock Relationships as senior academic tutor in psychosexual studies until 2017. Janice has taught on doctoral degree and training courses, presented at many conferences in the UK and abroad, and has published on a range of topics. These include sexual arousal and desire, pain disorders, biopsychosocial factors in sexual development, and neurobiological aspects of sexual responding. She was joint editor and contributor to *Sex, Mind, and Emotion* (Hiller, Wood, & Bolton, 2006), and co-wrote a chapter for the European-wide Syllabus of Clinical Sexology. Janice has a private practice in North London and is especially interested in the relevance of neuroscience in understanding sexual behaviour.

Introduction

Falling in love is a much longed for experience for many people in our society, and at certain life stages it may become a priority to find someone and begin to develop a romantic partnership. While films and poems describe the thrill of finding the object of passionate love, popular culture is also replete with books and articles on how to manage distressing couple issues. Seeking and developing a relationship is exciting, but after the early intensity the challenge is to maintain the intimacy over time: the pain of unmet needs and shattered beliefs when difficulties emerge is considerable. Why we fall in love with a particular person, how we make the choice, and what we really experience, are all sources of ongoing fascination. When we decide to share our life with another individual we take a significant risk, although it may feel like the right step at the time. Nevertheless, relationship problems can emerge at any phase. Faced with the task of working with a range of issues, psychosexual therapists have looked to an integrated model of therapy, as research and practice have enhanced our understanding of both sexual behaviour and treatment modalities. Therapy models typically combine psychodynamic approaches with behavioural exercises, psychoeducation, systemic techniques, mindfulness, and cognitive behavioural therapy.

Neuroscience has recently addressed the topic of romantic relationships, based on advances in genetics and brain scanning methods during the last twenty years. Increasingly sophisticated techniques such as functional magnetic resonance imaging (fMRI), and positron emission topography (PET) have highlighted which brain areas become activated during specific emotional states and behaviours, and have enabled research into the neurobiology of sexuality, love, attachment, and romantic attraction to grow considerably. Research has addressed various questions, including how the flood of emotions when romantic partners first meet becomes a stable bond; what underpins the chemical changes that transform early obsessive preoccupation into a secure loving attachment, and how do the emotional and voluntary behavioural systems in the brain link with genital changes? Connections between sexual activity, cognitions, and emotional processes have also been studied using sensitive hormonal assay equipment to measure the levels of identified hormones released from specific neural pathways. Results from this line of investigation have led to further understanding of the hormones circulating in the bloodstream during sexual activity and their impact on emotional responses.

Although as a topic neuroscience may appear antithetical to talking therapies, I see psychosexual therapy as an approach that can potentially address complex relationship difficulties more effectively when it embraces scientific advances, rather than relying solely on well-described techniques. I also think we can manage our interpersonal responses better when we have some understanding of how the brain works when we experience strong emotions such as excitement, urge, anger, and anxiety, and encounter problems with a partner. Research into other areas of psychological and behavioural distress, such as eating disorders (Steinglass et al., 2019), childhood trauma (Banihashemi et al., 2020), and assault (Giotakos, 2020), has explored how brain-based concepts could guide and advance treatment methods.

My aim here is to address the question of whether neuroscience can offer insights into what happens to intimacy between people over time, from initial meeting to staying together or parting, and including the possible, but not essential, stages of couple relationships. Some aspects in this book will not be relevant to every couple, and others have not been the subject of scientific scrutiny into human behaviour. Much of the early work on the neurobiology of relationships and attachment has emanated from extensive research into the mating patterns and sexual response of other mammals, especially those who form pair bonds, and whose subcortical systems of the emotional-limbic brain are regulated by hormones, with significant similarities to our own. By contrast though, humans have evolved complex neocortical structures in the brain for abstract thinking and problem-solving, which differentiate us from other mammals. Specifically, our prefrontal cortex creates higher mental processes, enabling a mind with conscious reflection, the awareness of personal identity and feelings, and the potential to make choices (Panksepp & Biven, 2012).

Human relationships are also endlessly complex, involving the pull of conscious and unconscious processes, societal expectations, and what Damasio (2000, p. 58) described as the challenge of applying reason to "the pervasive tyranny of emotion". In neurobiological terms, the application of reason depends on the ability of the prefrontal cortex, our region for rational thought and awareness, to modulate responses in the amygdala, where emotions are instantly appraised and translated into bodily states. At the centre of learning to manage emotions is the recent understanding of neuroplasticity—the formation of new neural connections and pathways in response to environmental input; and the concept of neurogenesis—the ability of the brain to grow new neurons. Therapeutic work facilitates neural network growth by providing a safe learning environment, and an emotionally meaningful context, for the co-construction of narratives. In Cozolino's view (2017) psychotherapists are applied neuroscientists who resculpt the brain's neural networks and promote neural integration, through empathy, behavioural experiments, and emotional attunement.

Oxytocin has now become recognised as crucial for emotional bonding, safety, and security between romantic partners, and also for the creation of caregiver–infant bonds. As we shall see later there is considerable overlap between these two brain states, with the clear distinction that romantic love also involves brain regions that are active in sexual arousal. Vasopressin differs only slightly in structure to oxytocin, and some functions are similar, but there are interesting gender differences, with men having higher plasma levels of vasopressin than women (Ishunina & Swaab, 1999). According to Panksepp and Biven (2012), oxytocin and vasopressin are social sexual peptides that encourage emotionally expressive traits, and moreover these traits typically show distinctions between men and women. Higher vasopressin levels in men promote competitive and aggressive behaviours, while oxytocin encourages more nurturing behaviours, often shown by women. These are gender-typical patterns only and reflect a biostatistical concept. Most individuals express a combination of traits, depending on unique developmental and environmental factors.

Romantic relationships must start with the first meeting, a recognition between two people that a connection is forming, moreover one that could be meaningful and rewarding. How this happens, why individuals are initially drawn to each other, and all this signifies about attachment, object relations, and unconscious hopes, is of great interest, but is currently beyond the scope of neuroscientific research. A theoretical explanation for how partner choice is made has been proposed by Marazziti and Baroni (2012). They suggest a rapid response in the amygdala, the brain's instant response centre, to assess emotional tone and danger when possible partners meet, which is then registered in the hippocampus. Emotional memories and early childhood experiences with caregivers are stored in the hippocampus, enabling the individual to select a partner who evokes positive mental states, according to the above theory. However, as clinicians we know that complex choices are often made based on unresolved developmental issues (Ruszczynski, 1992), so partner choice can also be potentially dysfunctional, as well as ultimately stabilising and health promoting. Perhaps the amygdala–hippocampus link is the neurobiological pathway for recognising a significant other who might connect us to developmental issues, whether the unconscious wish is to repeat what was good, or repair what was bad or missing. Nevertheless, the initial awareness that this person seems important is understood to create an altered mental state, characterised by elated mood and exhilaration. Methods now exist to explore this state scientifically, but empirical research can take place only after the initial recognition and sense of connection between two people has taken place.

Neuroscience illustrates the basic human need to connect to others, and how our thoughts, emotions, and behaviours—brain based activities reliant upon multiple neural pathways—underlie the nature of those connections. This book is therefore an attempt to give an overview of the neurobiological mechanisms involved in love, sex, and intimacy, and to consider how neuroscience has the potential to enhance relationships and psychosexual therapy through the insights offered from this expanding area of research. In the brief case vignettes at the end of each chapter I have tried to show how including neurobiological descriptions of psychological states can add depth to therapy practice. These vignettes are composites from my work over the years and are not intended to illustrate a complete treatment model. I suggest the use of the term neuropsychosexual, to describe an approach to sexual and relationship issues, that contains an understanding of brain phenomena and their role in the expression of love and sex.

CHAPTER 1

Starting a relationship: initial passion

Intense romantic feelings when two people first meet are often recalled as high points in relationship development. Certain experiences tend to be remembered clearly and may be looked back on long after lovers have established an ongoing bond: the first meeting, a sense of attraction and interest, the feeling that this person could be someone special. Early-stage romantic passion has unique features not found in the many other forms of love, such as feelings of euphoria, excitement, increased energy, and being highly motivated. Also, new lovers experience sexual desire focused on a single person, longing for union—emotional and physical—and proximity with that person, and the need for reciprocation. These powerful human emotions have been a central feature of art, literature, and culture over the centuries. Being in love is an exhilarating, joyous, but confusing emotional state; excitement and intense thinking about the new person may be accompanied by feelings of anxiety if desire is mutual as well as when it is not reciprocated. Obsessive thinking about the loved one, a central feature, can feel distracting but also underpins the wish for proximity. Being near to each other enables partners to get to know one another and develop a way of being together, and rearrangement of priorities often occurs. Hatfield and Sprecher (1986) have captured the main features of initial passion in their Passionate Love Scale, widely used in research, which was specifically designed to assess the cognitive, emotional, and behavioural components of intense early love.

In a significant piece of research into the impact of romantic love on neural processes, Bartels and Zeki (2000) used neuroimaging techniques to explore the brain systems that become activated with romantic love and to make a comparison with friendship. Blood levels increase when brain areas are activated, and this is indicated in scans by a blood oxygen level dependent (BOLD) signal revealing which specific areas of neural functioning are responding. Researchers asked subjects in an fMRI scanner to view photos of the partner followed by those of a friend. A unique set of interconnected areas in the brain's reward circuitry were found to differentiate the two sets of emotional responses. These brain regions include the ventral tegmental area (VTA), anterior cingulate cortex (ACC), insula, caudate nucleus, and the posterior hippocampus. Contrasting neural activation shown by participants in this study showed clearly how the brain separates romantic love from friendship.

Other researchers have used the same format to examine further why initial passion/romantic attachments in the early phase feel so uncontrollable and compulsive. In the first of a series of experiments Aron et al. (2005) repeated the above method, placing men and women who were "intensely in love" in an fMRI scanner and showing them pictures of their beloved, alternating with a picture of a familiar acquaintance. Subjects completed the Passionate Love Scale plus a measure to assess the general tendency to experience emotions intensely, in addition to in-depth interviews. Their results once again showed activation in the VTA and the caudate nucleus to which dopamine-containing neurons project. Although the couples in the Bartels and Zeki (2000) research had been together rather longer, the Aron et al. (2005) results were similar, indicating which brain areas underpinned the experience of intense romantic love. Rather than a specific emotion, the concept of early-stage romantic love as a motivational and goal driven state, associated with euphoria and anxiety, was introduced. Fisher et al. (2005) identified a specific neurotransmitter balance, one that mediates behaviour directed at a specific goal, focused attention, and response to novelty, as well as seeking and motivation, with a neurochemical balance of increased levels of dopamine (DA) and noradrenaline (NA). Serotonin (produced in the raphe nuclei) becomes lowered as part of the brain state identified with passionate love (Aron et al., 2005; Fisher et al., 2005). DA (produced in the VTA) and noradrenaline (produced in the locus coeruleus) act as stimulants, underpinning the strong urge and eagerness we experience when highly motivated to find out more about a person, place, or idea, and these neurotransmitters are involved with all our natural appetites and motivations. As well as activation of the high DA areas, Bartels and Zeki (2000) also noted an opposite response, namely deactivations in the right prefrontal cortex and amygdala. Amygdala and cortical deactivations indicate that emotional learning associated with sadness, fear, aggression (i.e. negative emotions) becomes non-operable, meaning that assessment and judgement about a partner—the ability to mentalize and assess intentions—is suspended. Joy and exhilaration are experienced in this phase, but the ability to reason may disappear, and unwise decisions can be made to commit to a relationship before allowing time to develop more knowledge of a potential life partner and of the specific dynamics of couple communications.

Why does falling in love produce such high anxiety and obsessive thinking to the point where feeling "lovesick" is a recognised state and is considered to be a stressful condition? Marazziti and Baroni (2012) speculated that the abnormally low levels of serotonin create a "transitory madness" which enables individuals to overcome neophobia (natural fear of the new) to form a bond for mating and security. With a special but non-related person, a new lover, we need to trust and feel safe, in order to develop intimate contact. Depleted serotonin also characterises people with obsessive compulsive disorder (OCD), indicating that this neurohormone underpins the drive to focus thoughts and energy on specific goals. In a new relationship it is a single person who may be overvalued and pursued. By spending intense time together in the early romantic phase two people can find out whether they want the relationship to continue, and decreased serotonin is part of the hormonal profile that determines this behaviour. When the serotonin levels of people in love and those with OCD were measured, they were found to be significantly lower in both those groups compared with controls (Marazziti, 1999). After twelve to eighteen months into the relationship serotonin had returned to normal levels, similar to controls, and obsessive thinking about the partner had also stopped, thereby linking lovers' obsessive ideation to temporarily reduced serotonin. In the OCD group, serotonin levels remained low, however, and obsessive behaviour was maintained, causing distress to the sufferer, compared with the exhilaration accompanying a new passion.

Increased anxiety is another common feature, despite the sense of desire, longing, and excitement at the beginning of a relationship. Studies of people who have recently fallen in love show that levels of serum cortisol (the hormone we produce when stressed) rise during early-stage romantic attraction compared with controls who are not in love (Marazziti & Canale, 2004). After twelve to twenty-four months researchers found that levels of this hormone returned to normal, and no difference was found in cortisol between the groups. In addition, the above research found changes in testosterone, so that levels become lower in men and raised in women. Falling in love was suggested to eliminate some differences between the sexes temporarily, or to soften some features in men and, in parallel, to increase them in women (Marazziti & Canale, 2004).

Human neurobiology works well in this phase, due to an elevation of circulating oxytocin (OT) during the early stages of a romantic relationship. OT is well established as a neuropeptide with a central role in social attachment, sexual behaviour, and affiliation. Increased OT facilitates trust, emotional connection, and bonding, while also reducing anxiety. People often experience anxiety when forming an intimate connection with an unfamiliar person, and increased OT at this stage has the function of decreasing cortisol circulation. Marazziti et al. (2006) found a positive correlation between high plasma levels of OT and the anxiety scale of the Experiences in Close Relationships questionnaire (Fraley et al., 2000). Without sufficient OT release the individual will be at the mercy of anxiety states that may impair or prevent relationships from happening and could intrude on the bonding process that allows positive feelings to emerge. Circulating OT has a predictive value too. Research with couples showed that high initial levels correlated with interactive reciprocity, defined as affectionate touch, positive affect, and social focus. Interestingly OT also differentiated between couples who were together after six months from those who split up at that stage of the relationship (Schneiderman et al., 2012).

Dopamine has a particularly significant role in the neurochemical balance of complex emotional and passionate love states. This is due to the link between OT and DA, which has been described as operating in a bidirectional manner, each one increasing the release of the other (Baskerville & Douglas, 2010). DA increases with novel experiences (Fisher, 2004) and new lovers experience a brain high as the relationship grows due to an oxytocin–dopamine rush (Brizendine, 2006). Sexual arousal is also higher when OT is raised, and lovers tend to experience more pleasure from sex in the early phases. Couples often recall how much they enjoyed sex in the first few months and years, and it is a brain state that people often wish to return to when time has passed. Those feelings of passion and exhilaration depend on the response to novelty and novel experiences, with raised DA, which occurs automatically in the establishment of an intimate bond, but thereafter can only be sustained with concerted effort by both partners.

Romantic love was previously viewed solely as a strong emotion but following studies with scanning techniques the phenomenon of being "in love" was considered to be a fundamental human mating drive—a temporary brain state associated with neural activity in the reward and motivation areas of the brain (Fisher, 2004). All countries where data on mate selection is available have recorded the multiple aspects of romantic love, and these appear to be universal. Increased empathy, emotional dependency, and changing priorities to fit in with a new partner are part of this phase (Fisher et al., 2006). Moreover, romantic love is suggested to have an evolutionary purpose, which is to direct attention and time on a specific mating partner, a chosen love object, for the purposes of procreation (Fisher, 1998, 2004). Social anthropologists take procreation as a basic premise of evolutionary theory due to the need for genetic continuity on the population level, but many people who have no wish to procreate may still desire sexual intimacy, and this can be maintained long after reproductive years. For the individual, however, whether straight, gay, bisexual, or transgender, choices will be made over the life course about whether or not to find a partner and develop a relationship that suits their own needs.

Fisher's theory also demonstrates how the three systems of lust (sex drive), romantic attraction (intense passion), and attachment (longer-term bonding) are neurochemically connected but are also

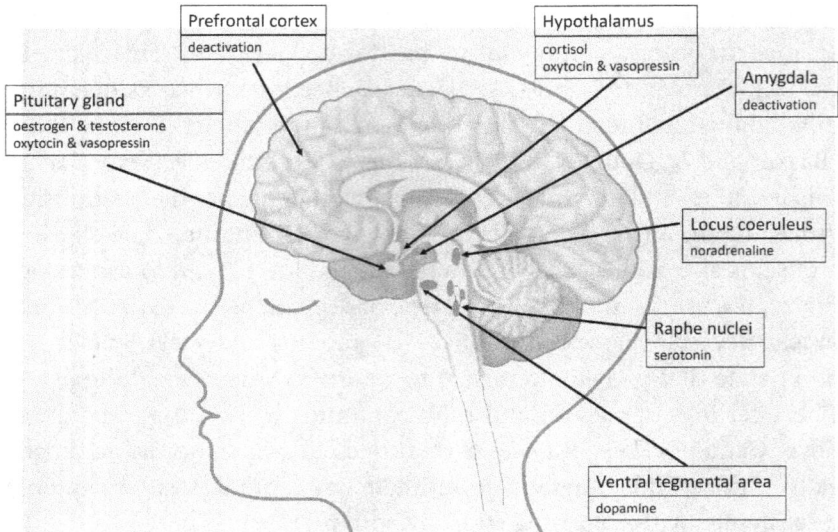

Figure 1 Diagram showing neural correlates of intense romantic attraction

With romantic passion, the pituitary gland stimulates the gonads to produce oestrogen and testosterone, powering lust and urge. A neurotransmitter balance of increased dopamine (DA) produced in the ventral tegmental area (VTA), and increased noradrenaline (NA) produced in the locus coeruleus (LC), creates motivation, excitement, energy, and drive. Decreased serotonin release from the raphe nuclei causes focused and obsessive thinking. Oxytocin (OT) and vasopressin (VP) are manufactured in the hypothalamus and released via the pituitary gland into the blood stream, for attachment and bonding. The HPA (hypothalamus–pituitary–adrenal) axis stimulates the adrenal glands to make and release cortisol into the bloodstream, increasing anxiety. Prefrontal cortex and amygdala deactivation suspends the ability to assess and make judgements about the other person.

discreet emotion–motivation systems. Lust, or a basic desire for sex is underpinned by circulating oestrogen and testosterone, but intense attraction to a specific person involves the pattern of raised DA and NA with decreased serotonin. Over time the bond to a conspecific other, or chosen mating partner, can evolve into a longer-term attachment; the association with OT and vasopressin has evolved to enable partners to stay together for child-rearing, purposes and security. OT and vasopressin, whose manufacture is stimulated by oestrogen and testos-terone, respectively, are the neurohormones required for attachment. These three systems can act independently or together, and herein lie some of the complexities of human relationships. Someone can love a long-term partner while feeling strong attraction for another and be tempted to seek out novel emotion-free sex while having sex with a valued partner (Fisher, 1998). Couples can also be committed to each other in the absence of sexual desire when that is satisfactory for both partners. Due to the separate activation of lust, romantic attraction, and attachment, humans have developed a range of reproductive strategies and mating behaviours that promote the maintenance of loving bonds but can also lead to intense disappointment and pain if hopes and desires are not fulfilled.

Summary and clinical relevance

Neurobiological research on early passionate love helps to explain why sex can be so much more rewarding and fun when people first meet. It also offers fascinating insights into why the personality traits of a lover at the start of a romance tend to change, or are experienced differently, after a period of time. Altering habits and adapting the self to please the other is a function of abnormally high DA and NA as part of early-stage emotional dependency. And feeling happy when making the other happy is an item on the Passionate Love Scale. However, once this phase has passed people tend to revert to their previous personality styles. We seem to have evolved neurologically with a tendency to overlook irritating aspects of the other's personality and habits and instead to focus on positive qualities when a relationship begins. As brain chemistry returns to pre-passion levels, negative behaviours can become sources of annoyance. A frequent complaint is that the partner seemed to have certain attributes or interests when they met (music/sport/hiking/gardening), or might agree to certain lifestyle choices (move to the country, have a baby), but these were not sustained, and eventually disappointment has set in. Finding out that someone we fell in love with does not have the qualities we thought they possessed or has changed their mind about a topic that matters, often leads to resentment and unhappiness and is a common reason for people to seek couple therapy. Describing how a temporary brain state can lead to adaptations that are not maintained might encourage more tolerance between the couple, rather than one or both feeling misled, or having a sense of aggrievement. This brain state also explains why people find time to see each other in the early phases but might struggle to prioritise the partner as time passes. Temporarily high DA and NA helps us to understand why people sometimes make rash decisions early on to commit to a relationship before taking time to get to know each other. In addition, high DA at the start increases OT release and facilitates sexual interaction and pleasure, but some people lose sexual interest once the novelty has gone, although the couple bond can remain strong on an emotional level.

Case vignettes

Hannah and Tom

Hannah and Tom, in their late twenties, came to see me after they had been living together for a year. Hannah wanted couple therapy because sex had decreased, and she felt Tom was not engaged with her needs in the way she had experienced him during the dating phase. This left her feeling anxious and insecure about physical and emotional aspects of the relationship. Tom was confused and upset by Hannah's complaints, and the couple were bickering over small things. For Hannah, Tom's support meant a lot as she wanted to progress career-wise before starting a family, and Tom agreed to this plan. Shortly after they began living together Tom found a new job which was challenging, and he gradually spent more time on his computer at home. Hannah tried to talk to him about the various work issues she was encountering but Tom seemed less interested in her and Hannah began to feel lonely. She rang her friends more often and went out with them occasionally as she used to before Tom moved in. Their sex life changed too. Rather than having sex three or four times a week as before, their sexual contact decreased to once a month on Friday nights. This didn't suit Hannah, who was tired after the working week, and preferred Sunday mornings, but Tom had started to go out drinking with his friends on Saturday nights and wanted to recover in bed the next day. Hannah cried and berated him when that happened, leaving Tom bewildered and attacked for seeing his friends.

In Hannah's background her mother complained frequently about being left to manage Hannah and her sister while their father spent hours involved with the local football team, which he coached. There were noisy rows between her parents, and Hannah felt angry with her father for his abandonment of the family. She accused Tom of being selfish and neglectful, which is what her mother warned her to expect of men. Tom came from a family where his parents took little interest in him. They both worked, had different household roles and separate interests, so he assumed Hannah would be accepting of how he spent his time. During couple sessions we talked through their different perspectives and disappointments, including how they both seemed to have projected family-of-origin issues onto their partnership. Hannah unconsciously hoped Tom would be different from her father and not become disinterested and absent, while Tom expected Hannah to be self-sufficient and repeat the space he saw between his parents.

Part of the therapy involved discussing the brain state of early passionate attraction, specifically how focused attention on the partner and motivation to find time to listen were linked to increased dopamine and noradrenaline. Eventually Tom accepted that he had not been available to Hannah in the same way since he became more absorbed in his own work, and that taking Hannah for granted was damaging. He started to listen properly to her job concerns as he had done at the start, rather than expecting her to know how much she mattered to him without any effort. Hannah realised she needed to regulate her emotions rather than express uncontrolled anger. They were encouraged to create a timetable or schedule for intimacy, which helps to build anticipation as well as desire, and is a useful approach to couple sex when spontaneity no longer works. Together they worked out how sex could happen at a time when they were both calm and in a relaxed mood, which improved their general relationship quality and decreased arguments.

Denise and Warren

Denise asked for psychological input because she very much wanted to become pregnant, but her partner Warren was insisting on using a condom during penetrative sex or having oral or manual stimulation instead. She was highly distressed, explaining that Warren had agreed to having a baby when they first met. His change of mind was causing her anguish. He had two teenage children from his first marriage, who Denise got on well with, and initially he said that he did want another child with Denise. Her ex-partner had been alternately volatile or dismissive, whereas Warren was calm and quiet. Denise had felt a sense of safety with Warren, who was forty-five and ten years older than her. She had always wanted a baby before she was thirty-five, partly to be different from her mother who was forty-three when Denise was born. She felt rejected and resentful at his avoidance of any sexual contact that could lead to pregnancy. When she became angry Warren would leave the bedroom, and eventually Denise also withdrew. They were hardly speaking when I first saw them.

Denise was the older of two children, and her mother became very depressed after the birth of her second child and was admitted to hospital with the baby for a few weeks. Denise stayed with an aunt, where she was lonely but couldn't go back to her father because he was unable to cope with childcare while working. Once home her mother continued to suffer bouts of depression, so family life was unpredictable and unstable for Denise. Warren had a very different upbringing in a strict home environment where his mother set the rules. He grew up resenting the way he and his father had to comply with his mother's dominating approach and spent most of the time alone in his room pursuing his own interests. Warren admitted he felt differently about having another baby after living together for a year, and Denise accused him of betraying her badly and tricking her into changing jobs and moving into an unfamiliar area to live with him. She cried in sessions, finding it hard to accept, but Warren was unmoved. He repeated that it was his right to change his mind. Denise was furious and said he lied to her, while Warren was quietly angry and remote.

Couple communication became stuck with the shared rage and confusion. They both seemed to want the other to repair their painful developmental experiences. Denise was desperate for a partner who was stable and could cope with her emotions, unlike her parents, whereas Warren wanted to control what he saw as unreasonable demands that would alter his way of life. In addition to helping them with their dysfunctional couple dynamic, I described how the neurochemistry of early romantic emotions creates a brain state which leads people to try to please the other and to mould themselves to be desirable. For Warren, Denise was an attractive woman who he fell in love with and who his children also became fond of, so he had intended for the relationship to work. However, once his brain state reverted he no longer had the strong impulse to please her, and the thought of a new family was stressing him. Explaining this process reduced the anger and disconnection sufficiently to enable the couple to talk about how to manage their opposing aims for the future. Denise could accept that her anger emanated partly from her insecure early home life, but she continued to feel very let down and disappointed over her wish for a baby. They ended therapy to see if they could work out how to stay together.

Neil and Stuart

Neil and Stuart were planning to move in together and asked for therapy because Stuart had become insecure and wanted regular reassurance. Both men were in their early twenties, shared many interests, and this was the first meaningful sexual relationship for each of them. They were very excited when they met and convinced it would last, until differences emerged. Neil was a gregarious outgoing person with a large friendship group—something that Stuart, who was much quieter, found very appealing at the start. He went out with Neil more than he was used to and joined in with the new people he met at parties and bars. Neil was drawn to Stuart's quiet manner which balanced his own extravert temperament. After a few months Stuart began to find the constant socialising too draining and preferred to stay in the flat he shared with his brother, while Neil, who lived with friends, continued his social life as before. Neil was upset about this as he wanted his boyfriend with him, and Stuart felt worried about losing Neil to someone else and expressed his jealousy. Neil found this oppressive, and they argued over their plans. Stuart accused Neil of thinking about leaving him, but Neil denied this, although he felt the suspicious behaviour might eventually drive him away. On their own they were still affectionate, with less sexual intimacy, which was a worry to both of them. Their greatest concern was whether the relationship would last.

Neil had one sister, much older than him, and his parents were reserved and quiet. They had very few social contacts and Neil thought his mother was lonely. He blamed his father and thought his mother was held back by his father's anxiety around people. Neil wanted fun in his life and thought Stuart wanted that too. He was angry with Stuart for not being as upbeat as he appeared to be at the beginning and turning into a stay-at-home person like his own father. In Stuart's background he was bullied at school and his family were disapproving when they found out he was gay. With Neil he had felt accepted and wanted for who he was for the first time and was very scared of losing him. They each accused the other of changing and of this being the cause of their problems.

Much of the therapy focused on misunderstandings and overreactions based on false assumptions. We also talked about how passionate brain states when partners first fall in love often lead people to attempt to please the other, so they might automatically adapt their behaviour to fit in with the partner. They were interested to learn about the impact of increased dopamine and noradrenaline, recognising the exhilarated emotions that dominated their first few months after meeting. Over time, as brain chemicals return to normal, the overwhelming desire to be who we think the other wants will gradually recede, and that is when a more careful evaluation of the relationship can take place. Thinking more about how both neurotransmitters and unconscious processes operate, helped Neil and Stuart to understand what they were projecting onto their relationship, and they began to see each other differently and to value what was good between them. Neil was able to express his feelings for Stuart, something that was lacking before, which helped Stuart's confidence and increased their sexual intimacy. Stuart eventually recognised his low self-esteem and started individual therapy to work on himself. As the tensions and miscommunications were untangled in sessions, both men felt stronger and more secure in their partnership.

CHAPTER 2

Kissing

A first passionate kiss is a powerful moment between two people. Frequently in films, books, and popular culture the kiss signals a turning point, as a physical sharing of bodily fluid, and suggests mutual attraction and further intimacy. In the early stages of a romantic relationship partners will probably have touched in some way before the first kiss—maybe handholding, a touch on the arm, or a hug to indicate growing closeness. Considering the emotional importance of open-mouthed kissing it is perhaps surprising that there has been very little research in this area until recently.

Researchers suggest that kissing is a way of receiving information—subconsciously—about the other person and may have a part to play in deciding whether to pursue further contact. For example, a study with a large number of college students has shown that a high proportion of women and men report a loss of attraction after the first kiss, suggesting it has a particular relevance in deciding how a romantic relationship proceeds. Women participants were much more likely to see kissing as a way of finding out about the partner's emotional commitment, and as a prerequisite for sexual contact, while for men it was more of a means to achieve sexual activity (Hughes et al., 2007). Moreover, the type of kissing varied according to the aims, with tongue kissing being linked more strongly to sexual arousal and closed mouth kissing having a stronger association with emotional intimacy and resolving conflicts. Using a new scale called "YKiss?", Thompson et al. (2019) found sexual/relational motives, such as initiating further sexual contact and expressing love, were the main reasons for engaging in romantic kissing, with goal attainment/insecurity issues as the second category.

How do brain systems receive feedback from a kiss to achieve these, albeit unconscious, objectives? Lips and tongues are extremely sensitive due to their large number of sensory neurons. When people kiss, these neurons, and those from the cheeks and nose, relay complex chemical messages to the brain. These messages are received in the somatosensory cortex, part of the forebrain, via five of the twelve cranial nerves involved in cerebral function. Tactile information is processed by the somato-sensory cortex to enable initiation of behaviours specific to the situation. Kissing also releases the neurochemicals involved in bonding, arousal, and stress reduction; levels of oxytocin rise, while cortisol levels drop. At the same time blood flow increases, providing a possible link between lower blood pressure and kissing (Walter, 2008).

Exchanging saliva has a role too, as this conveys similarities and differences in immune systems. Males tend to prefer open mouth kissing with salivary exchange, and Hughes et al. (2007) suggested this is a means to influence the woman's interest in sex, because hormones and proteins can enter the system through the mouth. Testosterone is found in saliva, and the mucosa membrane inside the mouth is permeable to this hormone (Dobs et al., 2004) so kissing provides a direct route for testosterone to enter circulation. Moreover, finding out if a partner has a different immune system tends to form part of the unconscious assessment of a mate, especially for women (Fisher, 2011). Mechanisms that discourage people from reproducing with a genetically incompatible partner would be activated by the chemical information transmitted during an open-mouthed kiss. Although research into the neuroscience of kissing is limited, the general conclusion is that the intense neurobiological connections convey subconscious information about the genetic compat-ibility of a prospective mate. Researchers agree that romantic kissing has a significant role in mate selection, due to the part played by kisses in the initiation of sexual arousal. Moreover, couples who continue kissing could be helping to maintain the bond in their relationship.

Summary and clinical relevance

Anecdotal evidence suggests that the majority of couples with psycho-sexual difficulties, especially an absence of sexual interest, have stopped kissing completely except for a peck on the cheek. If the role of kissing is partly mate selection and partly sexual arousal, the avoidance of passionate kissing would be expected when there is reluctance for intimacy by one or both partners. Absence of kissing also removes one possible route to feeling aroused and this will then compound a sexual difficulty. Many complex interpersonal issues combine to prevent intimacy, but raising awareness of the value of kissing as part of a psychosexual approach might help to unravel the defences and facilitate intimate exchanges. Reluctance to kiss can be addressed in gradual stages because underlying issues often require working through before this intimate shared connection can be possible and feel pleasurable again.

Case vignette

Lucy and Rory

Lucy and Rory, both in their mid-thirties had stopped having physical contact completely in the previous two years. Sex had been very limited after the birth of their first child, who was four when I first saw them. Rory expressed his misery and frustration at the lack of sex, which had worked well enough when they met but had never been very significant in their relationship. However, he could not tolerate a relationship with no sexual contact at all. Lucy had always been self-conscious about her body and experienced some serious medical complications during the baby's delivery. These were traumatising; she felt Rory did not understand what she had been through, and she was resentful that his life could continue while she had suffered. She wanted to be pregnant again but was not prepared to go through the intense stress she experienced at the prospect of intimacy. Both partners were extremely unhappy, but they wanted to stay together, and neither could contemplate splitting up.

We spent some time in sessions exploring the disagreements in their lifestyle that were causing distress, and working out how Rory could be more involved to give Lucy some time for her own interests. However, trying to introduce any contact beyond a brief hug created a deadlock in therapy. Although they had discussed their early experiences, I asked Lucy to describe in more detail what enabled her to be sexual with Rory in the first place. She remembered feeling relaxed when they kissed on the sofa for a few minutes in the first couple of months of their relationship, before she felt able to contemplate more intimate touch. This opened up a way forward, but Rory was very reluctant to return to what he thought of as "teenage behaviour". When I told him how kissing relayed important messages to the brain centres stimulating arousal he became more positive. Introducing some time spent kissing was useful for the couple, as Lucy began to enjoy feeling aroused. She could see how this helped her to contemplate sexual contact again. They moved on slowly to mutual touching exercises, called sensate focus, which enabled them to gradually increase sensual and sexual contact.

CHAPTER 3

Touch, sensuality, and attachment

Across many relationships from birth on, touch is important for the formation of social bonds, trust, and emotional connectedness. Holding and stroking a loved one is soothing, satisfying, and comforting, bringing immense pleasure to both the person being touched and the one doing the touching. For babies, the sensations arising from being lovingly held by the caregiver are considered even more central to healthy development than breastfeeding (Gerhardt, 2004). Mothers and fathers who are regularly involved in providing physical care with touch and play, will develop parent–infant synchrony, through the creation of neural connections in the prefrontal cortex, stimulating the reward centres to release dopamine (DA) and oxytocin (OT). In the absence of loving touch newborns and infants are at risk of social and emotional difficulties and may struggle to develop close bonds and friendships or may have more serious developmental impairments. Depressed levels of the hormones linked to communication and stress regulation have been associated with limited physical contact, as shown in the Romanian orphan studies. Adopted Romanian orphans were found to have lower levels of vasopressin (VP), associated with familial recognition, and also lower levels of OT than peers, after play with their mothers (Fries et al., 2005). Severe deprivation of human contact is speculated to produce stress-related high levels of cortisol bathing the brain, causing damage to receptors for OT and VP. Without enough receptor molecules these bonding neuropeptides will not be released for circulation. Researchers view touch as essential to mental well-being, and critical to thriving physically.

In adult life touch is also the platform for intimacy and sexual relations. Keltner (2009) describes the skin and hands as the medium through which we reassure, soothe, and convey emotional states such as sympathy, and love. Touch through handholding was found to have a powerful impact on neural activation to the threat of physical pain and also to reduce negative emotions, with the speculation that this effect was due to opioid release (Coan et al., 2006). And embracing a romantic partner also has an impact on stress responses. In a study designed to assess whether touch through an embrace, prior to a stressful event, could help to decrease the response to stress, researchers found that for women, embracing their partner did decrease circulating cortisol. Interestingly this stress-buffering effect was not shown by men in the study (Berretz et al., 2022).

On a neurological level, touch is relevant for the formation of social bonds because it triggers activation of the orbitofrontal cortex (OFC), the brain region in the prefrontal cortex that underpins an individual's search for basic rewards in the social environment. This brain region has extensive connections with sensory areas as well as limbic system structures involved in emotion and memory. When activated, the OFC sends messages to the hypothalamus, resulting in the release of endorphins and OT creating pleasure, safety, and trust: the emotional states that are needed to allow someone to become intimately involved with a new person. Pleasurable states also activate our reward centres so that DA release is triggered.

Physical exploration through stroking and touching as a relationship develops might occur before kissing but it is likely to take place with increasing excitement after partners have implied mutual interest. Films and TV shows in our present culture tend to show couples moving swiftly from a deep kiss to rapid removal of clothing for bodily contact, but progress towards intimate touch may well be much slower and more tentative in real life. Women in particular are thought to require a sense of trust with a possible romantic partner before moving to intimate physical contact. Hugs have a role here, because if they last twenty seconds they cause the release of OT and this activates the brain's trust circuits, while also increasing DA (Brizendine, 2006). In the right context, touch through hugging can increase the likelihood of more intimacy developing. Our response to touch, however, is very context bound. Touch from someone we do not know or like is experienced completely differently from touch by a loved one, and it is common to feel an aversion to being touched by someone we love, who in that moment has annoyed or upset us. Damasio (2000, 2010) viewed emotions as physical states arising from the body's responses to external stimuli and described feelings as mental experiences of our brain's interpretation of emotions. Aversive or unwanted touch sends messages to the medial orbitofrontal cortex (mOFC) and then to the amygdala, the emotional-limbic brain area that instantly assesses the situation, so if this alarm centre is triggered the wish for closeness will disappear. At other times when we do feel close to someone, being touched or held is very much wanted and may be calming, reassuring, or exciting, depending on circumstances. When touch from a lover is exciting the dopamine release can create a subjective state of desire for further sexual contact if both partners want to continue with lovemaking.

Throughout our lives physical contact in the right environment provides comfort and has anti-stress properties. Massage and certain alternative therapies have health-promoting effects due to the balance between cortisol, the stress producing hormone, and OT which has significant anti-stress properties (Uvnas-Moberg & Petersson, 2005). OT release plays a crucial role in maintaining emotional closeness, security, and satisfaction throughout the course of a relationship. In a study on the effects of massage on couples, participants who were healthy but experiencing stress were given a mutual massage programme to assess the impact on various measures, and the programme was shown to significantly decrease the perceived stress and to increase the mental well-being of participants, a change which was maintained at a three week follow up (Naruse & Moss, 2019). Sensual touch and mutual caressing, in the form of sensate focus exercises, have been a valuable psychosexual treatment approach as a first step to increasing sensuality for couples experiencing a range of sexual difficulties. Pacey

(2023) reported that certain couples for whom sensual touch with sensate focus exercises was considered to be appropriate found it a highly pleasurable enriching experience, and a way to reconnect when sexual interest was declining. Therapists in the study described the value of caressing exercises as a way to re-establish the relationship as a safe haven, while increasing attachment security. Research of this nature illustrates how behavioural exercises, like sensate focus, can be successfully combined with in-depth psychodynamic methods to address psychosexual difficulties, and a neuroscience perspective can offer an additional therapeutic approach.

Summary and clinical relevance

Research into the neural correlates of touch clearly confirms the value of guiding partners to gradually introduce, or reintroduce, some form of intimate physical contact. Clinical judgement, together with discussion with the couple, can identify when and how to increase touch as part of their interactions. On the level of brain systems, achieving a sense of trust is essential, so reducing negative emotions with couple therapy is often included as a first step to enable hugging, hand holding, or a limited form of contact to be received positively. Explaining the role of the prefrontal cortex, dopamine, and oxytocin to couples can aid this process. When partners are emotionally ready, moving treatment on to incorporate mutual caressing with sensate focus can lead to further cortisol reduction and OT release. This paves the way for specific techniques aimed at identified difficulties, as part of the therapy. Encouraging sensate focus exercises at the right time is one of the most significant features of an integrated treatment model in psychosexual therapy.

Sandra and Graham

Sandra and Graham had been living together for two years when they came to see me about the change in their sexual relationship. Sex had always been pleasurable and easy for the couple, but problems set in when conception became the focus. Sandra was in her late thirties and had always been unsure about having children. She met Graham online and they immediately felt a connection and attraction. Sandra was bright and bubbly with a positive approach to life. She thought Graham, at fifty-two, was more mature than her previous boyfriends, and the fact that he had two teenage children from his first marriage was appealing, due to her own ambivalence about coping with a baby. Graham was drawn to Sandra's outgoing personality and found her uncomplicated in comparison to his ex-wife. She also got on well with his children, which was most important to him, and she moved into his house quite soon after they met.

Initially Graham was also doubtful about having another baby, but as his business became very successful he realised he wanted a family with Sandra. In her background Sandra's father had died when she was five, and her mother really struggled to cope, with two older children and a low income. As the youngest Sandra played on her own a lot and felt she was left out in the family. She could see that mothering was very hard work and felt sorry for her mother being constantly exhausted. Sandra realised she didn't have the skills for full-time parenting. Also, she enjoyed her office manager job and was in line for a promotion, so she was most reluctant to give it up for childcare, which she viewed as daily drudgery. Graham reassured her that he could afford to get help with a baby and Sandra could go back to work whenever she was ready. Eventually he persuaded her to try for a pregnancy and they started to monitor her monthly cycle. Graham was very keen to have a baby as soon as possible and wanted sex morning and night during Sandra's ovulation phase. Although she was very aware of her age and worried about disappointing Graham, Sandra found herself unable to relax and respond, and had started to resent sex altogether. She wanted to please Graham but admitted to feeling like a potential baby container instead of a lover. Graham was worried that Sandra would become resentful and withdrawn. Both partners were upset and confused by the situation.

When discussing what was happening during sex, it emerged that Graham had become task oriented at the times Sandra was likely to be fertile and just wanted penetration. For Sandra, the playful few minutes with hugs and touch that they enjoyed previously had created a mood state in which she could feel desirable and appreciated, and then become aroused. Graham struggled to see how that mattered when they got on so well together. However, he was interested to hear how touch stimulated the OFC and hypothalamus to release oxytocin and dopamine, creating a sense of trust and safety with a partner. He thought Sandra should know that anyway as he trusted her with his children and home. Nevertheless, he agreed to alter his approach to sex and try a long hug and sensual touch whenever they had intercourse. This made a significant change and after a few more sessions Sandra reported being able to enjoy sex again. She also felt they had become closer and were communicating more about their sexual relationship.

CHAPTER 4

Sexual intimacy: arousal, desire, and orgasm

People are frequently concerned that sexual intimacy during the early stages of a romantic relationship is more exciting and has a stronger sense of urgency and drive compared with the experience in an established partnership, which can become formulaic. This change from enthusiasm for sex to maintaining routine intimacy is often distressing, for one or both partners. For other couples sexual contact was always a difficult area, becomes problematic, or disappears completely over time. This chapter addresses the brain phenomena that underpin sexual responding to increase our understanding of this complex area of human relationships.

Initially the experience of desire, which is a brain event, was thought to precede arousal, consisting of physiological changes, and the sexual response cycle was described as a linear model of desire, followed by arousal, and then orgasm. Since that original concept, sexologists have discovered that desire, or urge, and arousal are closely interwoven. Evidence has also emerged of considerable dissimilarity between men and women in how the brain and genitals are connected, and a new model of sexual responsiveness has been generated to reflect updated material. The incentive motivation model, described below, has implications for one of the main presenting issues for couples seeking help, namely incompatible sexual needs, where one partner has lower desire or avoids sex altogether. In addition, psychosexual therapy was advanced considerably when Basson (2001) described a non-linear model of the female sexual response cycle, providing an explanation for what clients were reporting in the consulting room. Clinicians had identified a pattern of gender differences within couples for many years, and the non-linear model offered a language to express the concept. In this model Basson clarifies how women, especially in long-term relationships, are more likely to experience responsive desire—a sense of being sexually wanted by the partner—rather than experiencing internally driven urges, which are more typical of men, and were previously thought to occur spontaneously. However, in their new notion of the sexual response cycle Laan et al. (2008) have argued that a sexual stimulus has to be perceived by the brain in order to activate subjective feelings of desire. They describe an incentive motivation model of sexual responding which concurs with clinical and research findings much more than a linear model. The incentive motivation model holds that for everyone, sexually relevant stimuli are necessary for sexual arousal and desire, while the behaviour that follows will depend on context and meanings. For women, however, sexual initiations may lead to negative feelings more often than is the case for men, who tend to feel positive about input that evokes arousal. Women's interest in sexual behaviour therefore depends much more on the whole situation.

Basson's model fits well with the incentive motivation description and illustrates that if circumstances in the relationship and context are positive, then atmosphere, words, touching, and kissing could start bodily arousal processes and feedback to specific prefrontal cortical areas. Women's conscious awareness of feeling wanted can lead to an interest or desire for sex. Basson (2001) described how the increased well-being of the partner, emotional closeness, the woman's own pleasure, and other potential benefits, serve as motivations for sex that activate the arousal cycle. Sexologists now think that physiological arousal in the genitals, which tends to be different in each gender, precedes the sense of drive or desire for sexual contact.

Central to understanding the link between feelings (brain phenomena) and responses in genital areas (bodily experiences) is the medial orbito-frontal cortex (mOFC), a brain region in the prefrontal cortex that receives connections from many other regions and is thought to represent reward and emotion in decision-making. According to Elliott (2000) the mOFC can select a course of action based on whether it feels "right" and can convey this to other brain structures involved in arousal. Specifically, the mOFC sends signals to the periaqueductal grey (PAG), an area of the midbrain involved with emotional responses, including defensive and fearful reaction. Links between the PAG, the amygdala, and other hypothalamic regions provide information enabling the PAG to assess the individual's sense of safety, or comfort, some of which may be outside conscious awareness. In a sexual context, messages from the PAG are sent to the pelvic organ stimulating centre (POSC) in the brainstem, which then, through long descending pathways, stimulates pelvic functions, including those involved in sexual activity (Holstege, 2016). This PAG–POSC system has control of the genital changes needed for sexual responses. For women these include vaginal lubrication, increased vaginal blood flow, and expansion of the vaginal passage, while for men, prostate and erectile responses are involved. In turn the PAG receives information regarding pelvic organ changes. These relay systems demonstrate how the individual's sense of safety and trust in the immediate environment, including the couple relationship, will be automatically and unconsciously assessed by the medial orbitofrontal cortex, and will directly impact the sense of drive and willingness to become aroused and engage in sexual interactions. In the absence of trust in the relationship, and especially if negative emotions are causing conflict, there is the risk of sexual contact decreasing or stopping completely, creating further stress and tension between partners (Hiller, 2006).

There are, however, distinct differences between the genders in terms of how genital responses are conveyed to the brain areas involved in decision-making about proceeding with sexual contact. For men the sensation of an erectile response is rapidly relayed to the brain, so the subjective experience of arousal then drives an urge for sex. By contrast, research using vaginal plethysmography—a device to measure the amount of blood in vaginal walls—has shown that women can experience blood flow to the genitals, called vasodilation, without feeling subjectively aroused (Laan & Everaerd, 1995). Low concordance between subjective feelings and genital changes was similarly confirmed in a later study, measuring genital arousal with pelvic MRI technology,

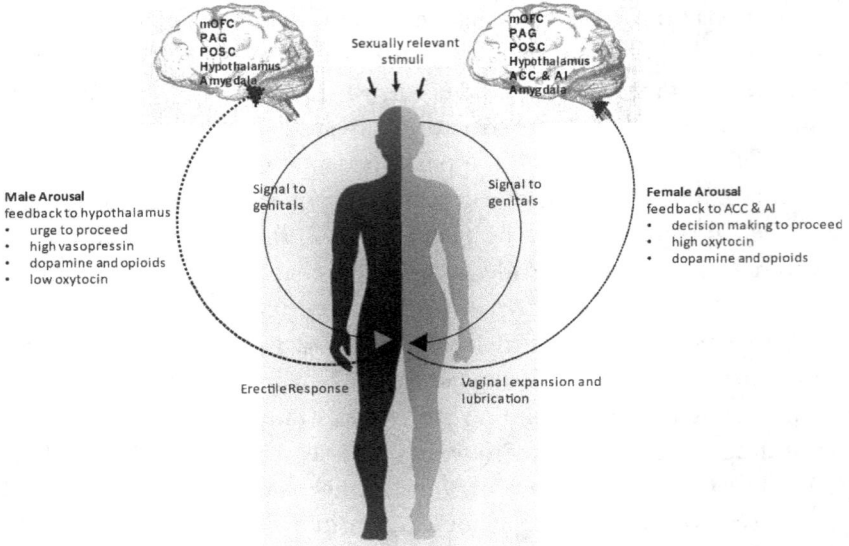

Figure 2 Neural correlates of sexual arousal: main brain regions and neurotransmitters

Stimuli are assessed by the medial orbitofrontal cortex (mOFC) and signalled to the periaqueductal grey (PAG), to assess "safety". The PAG then sends messages to the pelvic organ stimulating centre (POSC) in the brainstem to stimulate genital changes and receives information back about vaginal and penile changes. In men an erectile response indicating arousal is rapidly relayed back to the PAG, which is connected to the hypothalamus, ventral tegmental area (VTA), and amygdala. Dopamine, vasopressin, and opioids are released to underpin arousal and an urge to proceed with sex. Genital changes in women do not instantly convey arousal. Instead, the PAG, ACC (anterior cingulate cortex), and AI (anterior insula) become activated to enable decision-making on whether to proceed with a sexual encounter. Oxytocin, dopamine, and opioids will be released if the woman chooses to go ahead.

in a laboratory setting where women were shown erotic films (Heiman & Maravilla, 2007).

Neurobiological evidence has also supported the concept of dissimilarity in brain–genital links between women and men. Karama et al. (2002) showed erotic films to women and men when placed in fMRI scanners and compared the neural activation in this condition with what happened in the brain during the viewing of neutral film excerpts. Both genders had increased neural activity in the same regions when viewing erotic film excerpts, and these included the medial PFC, OFC, anterior cingulate, and amygdala. However, for men only, watching erotic films was correlated with activation in the hypothalamus (the brain area linked to sexual activity) and also with subjective levels of sexual arousal which the men recorded simultaneously. Links between the hypothalamus and amygdala when arousal occurs would appear to be central to how men and women respond to sexual cues, with men appearing to have stronger neural connections than women.

Individual and contextual factors are relevant in this area, and more recent research with women has highlighted awareness of changes within the body, called interoception, as playing a part in responsiveness to sexual stimuli. Handy et al. (2020) used a different statistical approach from Laan and Everaerd (1995) and found significant differences between individuals when physiological and subjective sexual arousal responses were compared. Looking in detail at variability between individuals, researchers reported that the women who were high on interoception also showed a correlation between physiological and subjective arousal when watching a sexual film. Further research on how this affects sexual behaviour is not available, but it seems probable that someone who experiences physiological feedback from genital organs, so their brain becomes consciously/subjectively aware, is more likely to want to act on those sensations than a person who does not experience those messages. At the same time, while some women do become subjectively aware of genital responses caused by vasocongestion, these are not the main motivating factors for engaging in sexual behavior, and neither is sexual fulfilment or desire for many women (Basson et al., 2004). Instead, women's sexual drive is understood to be motivated more by a wish for emotional closeness and connection, or to avoid tension in the relationship, rather than genital sensations or sexual fantasies. In contrast to women, most men find it difficult to achieve an erection in the absence of urge or desire (Leiblum, 2007).

We might expect that anxiety and stress would interfere negatively with arousal and there would be a straightforward connection between cortisol secretion and genital responses, but this is not the case. When people are stressed the hypothalamus–pituitary–adrenal (HPA) axis is activated to release a cascade of hormones, eventually causing the adrenal gland to release adrenaline and cortisol. Although cortisol does have a major role in regulating sexual arousal in men, fMRI research indicates a complex interaction between individual differences in sexual inhibition, mood regulation, and arousal. In a study of how cortisol was associated with brain activation during a sexual approach, researchers found a response in the mPFC and amygdala. Both these brain regions were activated, but the impact of cortisol seemed to depend on whether the man experienced arousal when anxious, sad, or angry, or is someone who used sex to cope with anxious feelings (Rodriguez-Nieto et al., 2020). In general, high anxiety levels in men tend to impair the erectile response, but some men find that engaging in sexual activity can help an anxious negative mood, possibly because the oxytocin released with orgasm can decrease cortisol levels and therefore reduce feelings of anxiety. Women show the same paradoxical effect of mood state on sexual desire. Individual differences in sexual desire seem to depend on many mood and relationship-related factors that can all influence sexual responsivity (Bittoni & Kiesner, 2022).

This applies to circulating cortisol in women as well. In a study examining women's sexual arousal levels in a laboratory setting, Hamilton et al. (2008) compared cortisol responses and genital arousal (measured by vaginal photoplethysmography) with a questionnaire measuring sexual arousal functioning in real life. Researchers found, as expected, that most women showed a decrease in cortisol when watching an erotic film. Some women, however, actually had increased cortisol levels with sexual stimuli, and this group were shown to score lower on arousal, desire, and satisfaction measures of sexual functioning on a validated scale. In a further study, Hamilton and Meston (2013) compared women with high chronic stress to those with average stress. Results showed that distraction from the stimulus was the main predictor of low genital arousal in the high stress group, while cortisol and distraction were both associated with low scores on arousal measures. Similar to men, it would appear that anxiety and stress in women, as indicated by cortisol levels, show individual variability, and raised cortisol can reduce sexual arousal and pleasure.

As we have seen, women are able to proceed with sex despite the absence of desire, but without sufficient vasodilation and vaginal expansion the attempt at penetration can be uncomfortable. If discomfort is extreme women can experience genito-pelvic pain/penetration disorder (GPPPD). This cluster of penetration difficulties consists of dyspareunia (pelvic pain during or after sexual intercourse) or vaginismus (an involuntary spasm of the musculature surrounding the vagina). Attempts to penetrate a closed vaginal passage will cause pain or will not be possible. GPPPD covers the main non-organic arousal problems for women, but at this stage there are no studies exploring the neurobiological underpinnings of these conditions. Based on what is known so far about the PAG–POSC link demonstrated in the Holstege (2016) study described above, the hypothesis would be that appraisal in the mOFC of the emotional and other factors relevant to the woman would determine the messages received by the PAG. Without a positive appraisal, the neural pathways facilitating blood flow to the genitals would be impaired and inhibition of vaginal expansion could then cause pain if penetration was attempted.

Arousal problems in men present as erectile difficulties. These are probably the most common and distressing issues that bring men to therapy, and an integrated psychosexual therapy approach will consider many aspects of the man's past and current sexual functioning (Binik & Hall, 2014). This is also where pharmaceutical products such as Viagra and Cialis are so successful. They belong to a class of drugs called PDE5 inhibitors, which work by inhibiting PDE5 (phosphodiesterase type 5), an enzyme that blocks the processes resulting in nitric oxide release. PDE5 inhibitors prevent the chemical breakdown of cGMP (cyclic guanosine monophosphate), a molecule that relaxes smooth muscle and leads to increased blood flow. During vasodilation in the penis, nitric oxide activates the synthesis of cGMP, and a product such as Cialis can increase cGMP in the smooth muscle cells and thereby prolong an erection to enhance the arousal process. Cialis is reported to act faster, last longer, and has fewer side effects than Viagra, although, as with all medication, individual responses can vary, and not everyone responds well. With a PDE5 inhibitor, anxiety or fear relayed by the amygdala to the HPA axis is bypassed, and the presence of an erection is relayed to the mOFC, where sexual desire is experienced. We can see why a drug of this kind would not increase sexual drive in women, which is more dependent on the relational context rather than genital vasocongestion.

Although emotional closeness is significant for men, male sexual arousal is far more sensitive to the processing of visual stimuli by the mOFC, where the stimulus is evaluated. Both the PAG and hypothalamus are connected to the mOFC, of relevance to arousal because research shows that oxytocin and vasopressin, produced in the hypothalamus, are central to becoming aroused, as described in studies below. Despite some discrepancies, the research overall indicates the involvement of an intricate network of brain areas underpinning the erectile response, with a central role for the nucleus accumbens and hypothalamus (Cera et al., 2012) which may explain the sensitivity of male arousal to disruption.

Differences in arousal patterns and cognitive awareness between women and men suggest that the genders typically face different challenges concerning sexual behaviour. Whereas the challenge for men is whether to act on an urge or to inhibit it, depending on contextual and societal factors, women more commonly choose to have sex with a partner for reasons other than having an urge for sex or feeling aroused, especially in long-term relationships. Pleasure from sex in both women and men depends on oxytocin (OT) release, which enhances opioid and dopamine release, and shows a surge during orgasm, although this may not happen simultaneously. For men who can control the urge to climax, the thrusting phase can last for seven minutes, or much longer on occasions (Brizendine, 2010). This means the timing of orgasmic release is something that couples might want to negotiate to reduce disappointment, as well as complexities arising from pain for the woman if intercourse continues for too long.

How can neuroscience contribute to an understanding of the links between physiological changes, sexual urges, and the cognitive appraisals of bodily states that guide human sexual behaviour? At this point we must turn to the numerous laboratory experiments with prairie voles. These small mammals form monogamous bonds for raising offspring and have yielded much information about mammalian pair-bonding, separation anxiety, mutual defence behaviours, and other aspects of social exclusivity, which are all shown by prairie voles, and not by other asocial promiscuous vole species. Research into the mating patterns of prairie voles has confirmed gender differences in the secretion of OT and vasopressin (VP) during copulation and bond formation. Specifically, the release of vasopressin during copulation is crucial for male prairie voles to become attached to a mate and exhibit mate-guarding behaviour, whereas when vasopressin is injected into female prairie voles, they reject attempts to copulate by males they would otherwise accept. Instead, females require oxytocin release during copulation to bond with a mate. Male prairie voles also lose persistency in sexual drive in the absence of vasopressin, while females whose OT receptors are blocked will attack males who attempt to mount them (Carter, 1992; Panksepp, 1998).

Testosterone levels in men decrease with age and there is a subsequent impact on drive, and reduced VP manufacture could partly account for the change, although this has not been verified. Circulating oestrogen levels decline gradually in women (as does testosterone) with well-documented changes in sexual response and desire. Manufacture of OT and VP in the hypothalamus is stimulated by oestrogen and testosterone, respectively, and they are released rapidly in the brain via the pituitary gland, providing a link between the physical environment and the needs of the organism. OT and VP are both crucial for the formation of attachments to caregivers and partners. And significantly for human interactions, social experiences during development can alter neuronal pathways for these neurohormones, and thereby influence emotional expression and bonding behaviour (Carter, 1992, 2017b).

Assessing the role of OT and VP in laboratory studies with mated animals has been invaluable, but similar research with human pair bonds has proved more complicated, because invasive methods are clearly not possible. Instead, investigations with human subjects involve self-stimulation, and studies have indeed highlighted differences between women and men in the pattern of OT and VP release during arousal and orgasm. Because both neuropeptides are released from the pituitary gland into the bloodstream, they can be measured by collecting blood samples in laboratory settings. Carmichael et al. (1987) assessed neurochemical changes during self-stimulation by regular collections of forearm blood, while various measures of genital blood flow, pelvic activity, and hormonal release were also recorded. OT levels increased during arousal in women and men, with a peak at orgasm. Of interest here is that the results showed that women had higher circulating OT levels during self-stimulation and at orgasm than the men, and OT release was linked to subjective levels of pleasure recorded by all the subjects. Murphy et al. (1987) studied self-stimulating men and also found a significant increase of OT during arousal along with a marked increase in VP levels, which dropped back to baseline levels with ejaculation, at which point OT release surged. This change in vasopressin levels in men has not yet been fully understood, but research with male rodents has shown how blocking vasopressin receptors rapidly eliminates drive and persistence for sex (Panksepp, 1998). VP is released during arousal in men so perhaps in the context of men's drive, vasopressin could add the dimension of persistence for sexual intercourse. Returning to male rodents, Panksepp and Biven (2012) describe VP as facilitating competitive and pushy behaviour. In men, staying power after orgasm is no longer required, and this is when levels of vasopressin have been shown to return to baseline. It is possible that vasopressin in humans has a similar drive function and contributes to the high arousal levels and sexual urgency experienced at times by men, although again this suggestion has not been verified. Increased OT secretion at climax in both genders has a significant bonding and attachment function, creating emotional closeness and trust.

A sense of safety with a partner seems particularly important for women's sexual needs in long-term relationships (Fisher, 1999). This area of research is consistent with the speculation that differences between women and men in the release of OT and VP could explain some of the variance in sexual drive and interest seen between the genders, an aspect of sexual relationships that frequently brings people to therapy (Hiller, 2004, 2005). From an evolutionary perspective women require security with a partner who will care for her and a baby if she conceives. After climaxing with a partner men tend to become tired and sleepy, partly as a result of the neurotransmitters released with orgasm. Increased levels of prolactin during orgasm, and VP during arousal, along with the release of melatonin, are thought to contribute to male tiredness following intercourse. Closeness and emotional attachment from OT release creates bonding with a female partner and enables men to take note of who they might be impregnating, especially if they wake up next to them, in order to protect and care for any potential offspring. Although some women complain about their partners falling asleep at a time when they want company, we can see that this aspect of male behaviour can have a valuable relationship function.

Pleasure from sex also depends on endogenous opioid release at the same time as OT secretion surges (Murphy et al., 1990), and the sensitivity of the brain opioid system is actually increased by OT. Opioid and dopaminergic pathways contribute to the stress-reducing properties of OT, which importantly has different functions depending on the context. Taylor (2006) found that young women in relationships had increased OT when experiencing distress with a partner and introduced the term "tend and befriend" to describe the role of OT in alleviating distress associated with meaningful social contacts, which occurs particularly in women. Male subjects in the Taylor (2006) study had elevated VP (and not OT) when experiencing distress. This outcome illustrates one of the many neurochemical contrasts between women and men. On the level of cognitive capacity Panksepp and Biven (2012) point out that the gender dissimilarities are negligible, whereas OT and VP underpin noteworthy differences in psychological and emotional traits, due to their impact on mental processes such as caring, seeking, fearfulness, confidence, and many other characteristics. Experiencing arousal is now seen as fundamental to having a desire for sex, but socio-cultural factors are highly relevant too and can profoundly impact the extent to which the individual is able, or allows themselves, to respond sexually. Yet another factor, in terms of the individual, is how someone feels about their own body, which can also influence the ability to respond to sexual cues (Poovey et al., 2022).

What happens in the brain during arousal and orgasm while couples have sex is a question that researchers are keen to explore using neuro-imaging and PET techniques, although the study of couple sex has not been achieved so far due to technical reasons, namely the need to be still in a machine. Nevertheless, placing subjects in scanning equipment while they self-stimulate or are stimulated by their partner, has achieved significant results. Dopamine (DA), the reward, anticipation, and motivating hormone, cannot be measured reliably in blood samples, and instead the role of DA is assessed by observing which brain pathways become activated during sexual activity. DA has several functions in the brain, including the suppression of both anxiety and fear responses in the amygdala when circulating at high levels. Of relevance to arousal processes is the DA–OT link, which operates so that high DA leads to the anticipation of reward with increased excitement, and higher OT levels reduce anxiety and inhibition, facilitating trust and bonding in relationships (Baskerville & Douglas, 2010).

Activation of DA-synthesising neurons originating in the ventral tegmental area (VTA), part of the lower brainstem, was demonstrated by Holstege et al. (2003) using PET imaging to measure brain changes in men during ejaculation while they were stimulated by their partner. A similar activation of the dopaminergic system was shown in women, this time using fMRI scans taken during orgasm (Komisaruk et al., 2008). When female subjects were stimulated by partners the neuro-imaging showed the nucleus accumbens of the forebrain becoming active. DA is transported from the VTA to the nucleus accumbens via what is called the mesolimbic pathway, indicating that DA is one of the main neurotransmitters with a key role in arousal processes involved in the build-up to, and during a climax. The mesolimbic pathway also transports DA to the amygdala (for emotional processing) and the hippocampus (for memory storage). Thus, DA release in this system might be part of the explanation for how we remember whether a certain sexual behaviour or person was rewarding and caused pleasurable sensations and experiences, which we will then want to repeat.

We might expect to see many brain regions becoming switched on, or activated, during arousal and orgasm but a rather striking outcome has emerged in further research concerning the opposite response, showing areas of the brain that were switched off or became deactivated. This indicates certain cerebral functions that are not required or might in fact impair sexual responding, a topic of relevance to clinical work, where we find individuals whose loss of interest in sex causes serious distress and couple disharmony. Placing subjects in PET scanners to study brain functions when women and men were stimulated to orgasm by their partners, Holstege and Huynh (2011) found the total deactivated brain regions in all subjects were much larger than the activated regions and were mainly on the left side. Left hemisphere functions include rational and analytic thought, planning, logic, and verbal skills. By contrast activated cortical regions were mainly on the right side, the hemisphere involved with emotion, intuition, creativity, imagination, and impulsiveness. Spontaneous emotional processing continues in the cerebellum which is located where the spinal cord meets the brain, as indicated by strong increases in blood flow in this region during arousal and orgasm

(Holstege et al., 2003). Prefrontal cortex deactivation was also found to be associated with ejaculation (Stoleru et al., 2012).

Taken together these results suggest that rational thinking, alertness to surroundings, and control of feelings (left brain activation) is downgraded during sexual stimulation and orgasm, whereas allowing the experience of emotions, spontaneity, and imagination (right brain activation) is part of the sense of "letting go" that happens as arousal progresses. Notably, deactivation of the amygdala—the alarm, fear, aversion, and aggression region of the medial temporal lobe—was a significant aspect of brain changes during orgasm in the Holstege and Huynh (2011) study. Recall that Bartels and Zeki (2000) also found amygdala deactivation when individuals were in the early passionate phase of a relationship and described this as impeding logical thinking and the ability to assess a partner rationally when initially in love. Both orgasm and being in love seem to be underpinned by brain mechanisms that switch off judgement and remove fear of the other.

Another part of the Holstege (2016) study compared women with lack of sexual interest, classified at that time as HSDD (hypoactive sexual desire disorder), to a control group by asking participants to watch erotic movies while in a PET scanner, and significant differences were found between the groups. Decreased neuronal activity was observed in the medial orbitofrontal cortex of women with absent or low desire compared to controls. Low desire women also had an absence of PAG activation, indicating that no messages were received by the POSC, which would explain the lack of arousal. Furthermore, the left side of the brain in this group was not deactivated, suggesting that alertness to surroundings was still present. Holstege (2016) speculated that women with low desire processed the watching of erotic movies as negative and did not block out other thoughts or awareness of the experimental conditions. This view concurs with Brizendine's (2006) description of how women need to relax and feel safe to avoid a strong amygdala response, and the suggestion that female sexual responsiveness requires a brain turn-off for women to become turned-on. From the Holstege (2016) PET scan study of women with low or absent sexual desire we can see which brain areas cause disruption of the delicate neuronal and neurochemical balance that is required to avoid distractions and enable the subjective experience of arousal.

Scientific research often produces anomalies, however, and a different study, this time using fMRI scans, found an alternative pattern of responses. Wise et al. (2017) placed women in a scanner to observe the brain regions involved in orgasm achieved through self- and partner-induced genital stimulation. Certain technical difficulties were overcome by minimising head movement with a custom-fitted thermoplastic whole-head and neck brace stabiliser. In contrast to the PET scan results above, there were no deactivated areas; rather researchers were able to see widespread activation of many brain regions at different rates before, during, and after orgasm. This fMRI research contradicts the PET scan results showing left brain and amygdala deactivation, and indeed clinical experience with women who lack interest in sex. A possible explanation for this contradictory finding by Wise et al. (2017) could be the nature of the final ten women who participated. The researchers report that another two women were unable to orgasm in the scanner so were excluded, although all participants previously described themselves as "highly orgasmic", as would be necessary for a study of this kind. Nevertheless, the requirement of having an orgasm when wearing a mask that was rigidly clamped to the scanner head cage was not achievable by all. Perhaps the ten women who could orgasm in those unusual experimental conditions had such strong responses and were so immune to their surroundings that brain deactivation was not essential.

Clinical experience and research have shown that female responsiveness varies considerably depending on context, environment, and individual differences. Some women are more likely to climax with a partner when early passion is strongest, while for others a committed relationship with a sense of safety sets the scene for orgasmic release (Brizendine, 2006). Similarly, it seems possible for certain women to become aroused and climax in a scanner with a head brace, while others are unable to do this. The women in the above fMRI study may therefore have been unrepresentative. Evidence suggests that most women do need to lower alertness to context and immediate surroundings in order to focus on their physical sensations and reach an orgasm.

Reviewing neuroimaging studies in the five years up to publication, Ruesink and Georgiadis (2017) highlighted some inconsistencies in the outcomes, but their analysis did concur with the concept of amygdala deactivation for a sexual response to progress. Moreover, decreased temporal lobe activity during high arousal emerged in numerous studies, which suggests that personal memories and factual knowledge are not part of this process. This review also cites the clinical results that over-control and inhibition (increased activity in prefrontal areas) were found in subjects with low or absent sexual interest, confirming that executive planning, social control, and self-regulation need to be within an optimal range for healthy sexual functioning to take place. The authors make the point that the ability to inhibit or control a sexual response is as necessary as the ability to respond, so the brain manages an optimal balancing of neural systems to allow us to make decisions regarding whether to proceed with sexual activity.

So far we have looked at the increased circulation of oxytocin and vasopressin in self-stimulating individuals or mated animals but assessing the role of these neuropeptides in human pair bonds has proved more complicated. Acevedo et al. (2019) devised a study that managed to do that. They investigated the genetic and neural correlates of individuals who were pair-bonded by taking DNA samples, examining brain scans, and gathering details of sexual satisfaction. Participants were scanned in fMRI machines to compare neuroimages when viewing the partner and when viewing an acquaintance, and areas rich in oxytocin, vasopressin, and opiate receptors showed strong activation for subjects viewing photos of their partner. Researchers were also able to demonstrate the role of higher order cortical systems underpinning cognitive processes unique to humans, such as awareness, meaning-making, empathy, and self-other processes.

We clearly have the capacity to self-regulate and to contain the strong automatic drives that other mammals are governed by, but the neurobiological evidence for the brain areas involved had not been previously identified. Acevedo et al. (2019) found activation in specific brain regions (parts of the PFC, temporal and parietal lobes) confirming how humans are uniquely able to combine unconscious automatic responses with thoughtful conscious choices in order to manage sexual urges. In addition, the results linked sexual satisfaction scores with specific OT (G-alleles) and VP (long-alleles) variants that have been identified as central to complex social behaviours such as trust, intimacy, and altruism.

Neuroimaging techniques have deepened our understanding of brain processes and sexual responding with a range of healthy subjects, and in addition research has shown that male and female brains generally have gender typical patterns whether the individual is gay or straight. For example, fMRI studies using appropriately arousing visual stimuli found similar neural networks were activated by gay and straight men (Kagerer et al., 2011; Stoleru et al., 2012). Similarly in another neuroimaging study involving gay and straight men and women, the men were shown to generally have stronger responses to visual stimuli than the women participants, who had less specific arousal patterns, and again there were no differences between gay and straight participants (Sylva et al., 2013).

Research with transgender persons is still in the very early stages, and there is a paucity of information on the neural correlates of sexual arousal and sexual satisfaction after transition. In a study investigating the neurobiology of cisgender and transgender persons when viewing sexually arousing visual stimuli, cismen, ciswomen, transmen, and transwomen were compared along four components of sexual arousal: cognitive, motivational, emotional, and the autonomic and endocrine components (Mueller et al., 2020). Neuroimaging showed that cismen had higher physical arousal and higher patterns of activation in specific brain regions within the emotional component than the other three groups, and overall showed notably increased responses in most of the areas and components. Many results were reported, but of note transmen were more similar in the emotional component to their sex assigned at birth and had less activation to erotic videos than cismen. Also, transwomen had reduced brain functional connectivity in attention and motivation areas compared to cismen, but increased connectivity in inhibition, cognitive, and emotional areas. Researchers looked at the role of hormones and brain regions linked to awareness of sexual arousal and pleasure and were surprised to find negative correlations for oestrogens in transwomen and testosterone in transmen. This differed from the positive effect of testosterone on cisgender men, while for cisgender women, oestrogen levels were not associated with sexual arousal. An earlier study on a large cohort of transgender persons found that hormone treatment for transmen caused initial increases in sexual desire, but these returned to baseline after three years. For transwomen though, despite an initial decrease in desire, retesting after three years showed greater sexual desire than baseline measures (Defreyne et al., 2020). More data will no doubt emerge in this complex area, but, at present, knowledge of how gender-affirming treatment and subsequent brain changes might impact on sexual pleasure or distress for transgender persons is still very limited.

Asexuality, defined as a lifelong absence of sexual attraction, has also received some attention in the literature, with unexpected results. Despite asexual persons reporting low, but not absent sexual activity, and low desire for sex, research into brain–body links showed that asexual women at least had normal physiological changes when viewing erotic films, similar to women who were not asexual. Interestingly the asexual women had higher concordance between genital responses and subjective arousal than the control group but did not experience this as a positive emotional state (Brotto & Yule, 2011). A similar result emerged in the only fMRI study that has been carried out to date, and this was with an asexual woman who viewed a sexually arousing film and a neutral film. By contrast with women who do have sexual interest, the asexual subject showed no activation in the anterior cingulate, amygdala, or thalamus when watching the sexually explicit film, and there was no neural evidence that she was trying to conceal her arousal: efforts to block arousal would be shown by prefrontal cortex activation. Researchers hypothesise that sexual stimuli are not recognised as arousing by asexuals, so a sexual response does not occur, while at the same time the cues are not experienced as threatening (Prause & Harenski, 2014).

Summary and clinical relevance

Difficulties with arousal and desire for sexual intimacy are a common reason for seeking therapy. People are often puzzled and distressed when their body does not behave the way they want it to in sexual encounters. Both women and men, with same sex or opposite sex partners, are at risk of losing sexual interest/desire when feeling angry, resentful, or hurt. Sometimes people are aware of the context, but equally these negative emotions may not be available to conscious awareness. Careful assessment of the unique factors in each case is important to devise an approach that addresses individual differences.

Neuroscience can now offer some insights into the brain-body system that enable or inhibit a response to sexual cues, by showing how the brain evaluates our mental state, the relationship, and other contextual factors, and relays this information rapidly to the genital organs. Specifically, the medial orbitofrontal cortex will send messages to the amygdala and hypothalamus, to the PAG and then on to pelvic areas, so that arousal towards the partner may be impaired if negative emotional states interfere. However, we are not consciously aware of this intricate process, and some benefit can be gained from knowing that the brain–genital connections are involuntary, but they can be altered through therapy to address conflictual areas in the couple dynamics.

Absence of sex as a result of hostility is based on anger and disappointment, rather than linked to anxiety. On an emotional level, women in particular tend to avoid sexual contact when feeling ignored, belittled, and undermined by a partner. The syndrome of low desire or loss of sexual interest is now called female sexual interest and arousal disorder (FSIAD). Some women choose to avoid disappointment and hostility in the relationship by having sex with a partner who has higher sexual needs. This is another way of reducing disharmony in the context of emotional management, but one which risks a build-up of further resentment. Women can continue to have sex without pleasure, although as described above, women may feel subjectively aroused once touch and foreplay has begun. Men, in my clinical experience, are particularly sensitive to repeated criticisms and angry outbursts, leading to a sense of failure and having disappointed a partner. In this situation they are generally unwilling to attempt sexual initiation or engage in sex if approached. Whatever the cause, the presence of strong negative emotions of any kind can disrupt sexual activity in the couple relationship and addressing these emotions will be a first step in the treatment process. (Sexual desire can, however, be expressed elsewhere, as we will see when infidelity is discussed in Chapter 7.) Finding a way to explain these brain systems can set the scene for therapy aimed at reducing hostility. Once negative emotions have decreased, physical contact and sensate focus may be appropriate. Physical contact with a partner increases oxytocin release and reduces cortisol, which enables arousal processes that could otherwise be inhibited. Increased DA enhances excitement and is also a brain state that reduces amygdala activation, so encouraging couples to include new activities into their lifestyle remains a positive approach.

Arousal disorders occur when underlying anxieties are impairing blood flow, leading to erectile difficulties in men, and vaginal pain in women due to lack of expansion when penetration is attempted. Feeling safe and secure with a partner increases oxytocin release and reduces cortisol, which enables arousal processes that could otherwise be inhibited by anxious thoughts. Describing how these neurotransmitters can block arousal gives a basis for the exploration and management of anxiety. Staying in the present and taking gradual steps towards increased sensual and sexual contact will be a part of the process. If appropriate, sensate focus exercises can be introduced with specific techniques, depending on the issues. As sensual touch increases, women may become distracted by various strands of thinking: these can include negative thoughts about the partner, involuntary memories of previous damaging experiences, distressing events, or lists of chores. If trust and emotional closeness are achieved, techniques to reduce alertness to surroundings by turning off left hemisphere awareness of external events are relevant here to encourage staying in the moment and focusing on bodily sensations. Men also become distracted by unwanted thoughts, although these are more likely to involve anxiety about their erectile response, and problems connected to work. Forms of negative thinking that undermine confidence and cause nervousness can seriously impact arousal and lead to avoidance. Guidance to focus on sensations in the moment with psychosexual treatment approaches can help people to decrease anxious states, and regain confidence, and any method that reduces amygdala activation can be suggested. Appropriate and caring touch has a clear role in reducing anxiety, confirming again the value of sensate focus exercises for specific psychosexual difficulties when appropriate for the couple.

Case vignettes

Haley and Philip

Philip requested couple therapy to address the absence of sex with his partner Haley. The couple had booked a wedding for six months ahead, but Philip admitted he was now having serious doubts about getting married and was very upset at the impact this would have on him and his children. They had met at a mutual friend's party, when Haley was forty, and recognised each other from the same school although Philip was two years older, so they had different friendship groups. They found out they were both recently divorced, and quickly developed an exciting relationship. Their sex life was spontaneous and "torrid" for more than a year. Haley had two children who lived with her, but she was able to stay with Philip at the weekends when his child was with her mother. All the children seemed to get on well, and the couple decided to live together with a view to getting married the following summer. However, once they shared a home and started wedding plans, Philip found himself rejected by Haley, which had not happened before. Haley was very excited about the wedding and determined it would be a much more successful experience than her first one which was a rush due to an unplanned pregnancy. Philip was less interested in the wedding and more worried about the cost. He worked in his father's business with his sister, and his parents were not pleased about the elaborate plans. Haley was angry with his parents for becoming involved and asked Philip to get his mother to stop questioning her about expenses. This caused disruption and tension between his parents and Haley. Philip was very torn as he did not want to upset any of them, but Haley thought she should be the priority. She was furious with Philip for not protecting her, and felt he was disloyal. Their relationship became very different from the mutually passionate one they had when they first met, but Philip was at a loss with how to repair the situation. He wanted Haley to put the disagreements behind her, but Haley became more upset at this suggestion. Philip knew his parents would respond badly if he asked them to stay out of his life and could not understand why Haley was unable to put her anger to one side and respond to him physically.

We talked about the impact of anger on the sexual response cycle, specifically how the mOFC judges the situation and relays messages to the amygdala, which reacts to perceived threats, anger, and danger. Since Haley had become so angry with Philip and his parents, her prefrontal cortex and amygdala responses had sent messages to the brain centres involved with interest in intimate connection and assessed this to be emotionally unsafe. Forgetting about anger is not possible once this feedback loop is activated, and the couple were able to see that the initial challenge was to address anger reduction and the wider family dynamics. This involved Philip reassessing his relationship with his parents in this phase of his life. He decided to stand up to them and ask them, especially his mother, not to interfere so that he and Haley could make the wedding arrangements on their own. For Haley, regulating her angry reactions was also an important part of the therapy, which she was able to do once she felt prioritised. They worked on their relationship issues for some months, and resolved the situation so that it eventually became possible for the couple to resume sexual contact before getting married.

Mike and Brenda

Mike and Brenda were in their early sixties and had both left their marriages and children to live together. Brenda wanted couple therapy because Mike had stopped responding to her approaches for physical contact and had become increasingly withdrawn. They each had two children who were all in their thirties at the time of therapy. Mike and Brenda had originally started a work affair which lasted for five years, until Brenda decided she could not tolerate her unhappy marriage any longer. She left her husband, rented a flat, and persuaded Mike to tell his wife and move in with her and her children. He had been reluctant to leave his children, predicting accurately that their mother would turn them against him, and he continued to feel immensely guilty about what had happened. Mike was unable to explain his lack of sexual interest as he had always been quite sexually driven in the past, and still had morning erections occasionally, but not with Brenda. At Brenda's insistence his testosterone level was checked and found to be within normal limits for his age.

It soon became apparent in the sessions that Brenda was very critical of many aspects of Mike's behaviour as well as the lack of sexual contact. She complained about his procrastination, remoteness, and in particular his avoidance of speaking to his children, who he rarely spent time with. Mike had no response to these criticisms but became upset and confused. It was difficult to get this couple to accept how these negative conversations impacted Mike's sense of trust and confidence in Brenda. Her complaints confirmed for Mike that he had done everything badly and let his children down, which partially explained his reluctance to see them. Before addressing the sexual relationship, we spent some sessions on what needed to happen to enable Mike to regain some confidence. We talked about the connection between his amygdala, which was reacting to the fear of getting things wrong, and his body's inability to become aroused, and therefore to have sexual urges. I suggested that when Brenda approached him for sex, his negative mindset prevented him from responding. He began to recognise the deep sense of failure he felt towards his ex-wife and his current partner. Although it was difficult for Brenda to accept her role in reinforcing his shame, this way of thinking about what had happened seemed to help her accept that pressurising Mike was not the way forward. Instead, we worked on rebalancing their interactions and focusing on how non-demand handholding and hugs could bring them closer. Gradually the couple moved on to full body contact but with underwear, as Mike was self-conscious about his lack of erection and refused to be stimulated or touched. He struggled with feeling this would be enough for Brenda and found it difficult to manage his conviction that he was a disappointment. He also refused to consider using Cialis or a similar medication to facilitate an erection. Brenda tried to persuade him that she liked the closeness and could accept the situation as it was. Mike found this concept difficult, although he wanted to believe her. They did achieve increased understanding of their relationship before they agreed together to end therapy.

Dean and Toby

Toby wanted couple therapy to address the difficulties he and Dean were experiencing with sexual contact. They had lived together for only ten months and the change in their relationship was distressing him. Dean, at thirty-five, was six years older than Toby, and had lived with a previous partner for a year some time ago. He put long hours into his work. Whereas Toby was openly upset about the lack of sex, Dean found it hard to express his emotions. It emerged that although he still found Toby attractive, there were aspects of their domestic arrangement that had disappointed him. He had hoped Toby would be more ambitious, find a better job, and be less dependent on him. For his part Toby was quite content living in Dean's house, which was much more comfortable than his previous flat share, and he liked cooking the meals. He was not in a hurry to change jobs and enjoyed socialising with Dean's friends. Toby found close contact in bed comforting and attempted to cuddle up to Dean at night before falling asleep, but Dean felt oppressed and trapped. He had grown up with a single mother, who was exhausted from working at two jobs, and younger brother who was quite reliant on him. Dean had to take care of his brother when their mother was not around, and the boys shared a bed until Dean left home at eighteen for college. His brother's neediness and reliance on Dean had created a dilemma that he was not totally aware of, as he wanted to be caring and supportive. At the same time, he desperately wanted to get away from his family to continue his education and develop his career. While he was very drawn to Toby, the domesticity appeared to trigger his wish to escape.

As part of their therapy, we discussed Dean's negative reaction to being very close to Toby in bed, and how this was not a rejection, but an involuntary response linked to sharing a bed with his brother for so many years. Toby struggled to understand and continued to express how unloved he felt. Dean was able to reassure him up to a point, so I helped him to see that Dean's brain was reacting to his brother's neediness, through long established neural pathways, rather than a deliberate rejection of him. It made a big difference to Toby to think about brain processes that we are not immediately able to control. The couple also raised the possibility of watching porn together for a brief phase, which was something they both wanted, in an attempt to kick-start Dean's arousal response. I talked about the link between the visual and sexual circuits in the male brain, which are more relevant to some people than others, and they decided to try that approach. Eventually Toby felt less wounded, and Dean learnt to express his emotions more, enabling the couple to become closer, with increased physical and sexual contact.

James and Penny

James and Penny requested therapy to address the absence of sex in their relationship due to Penny's pain when intercourse was attempted. They were in their mid-twenties and sex had always been problematic. Penny had avoided sexual contact previously, but they hoped the issue would change once they were married. After two years the difficulty remained, and they finally decided to seek help. Penny was from New Zealand, and left to get away from her problematic family, finding life in London liberating and exciting. She was the oldest daughter of four children with a father who was absent while running his business but was nevertheless a controlling presence when at home. Penny was aware of his sexual demands on her mother, who complained about his high sex drive, and how she struggled to manage. There were strong hints that her father had affairs when out of the country. From her teenage years Penny had stepped in to cook meals for the family because her mother used alcohol and tranquillisers when stressed and went to bed unwell. Penny was convinced that her mother's decline was due to her father's infidelity, which was never admitted, although her father left home for another woman soon after Penny graduated. She remained very supportive of her mother and angry with her father, refusing to have further contact with him. When she met James at work she was attracted to his solid character and strength, believing he would "be there" for her.

James had been sent to boarding school from the age of seven and was reserved and quiet in the sessions. He described his childhood as lonely with strict routines. His mother was controlling and orderly; his father was hard-working and absent. Although he was very unhappy at boarding school, he told no one and stuck it out. From an early age his mother complained constantly about his father's neglect of her whenever James was home. He would sit in his bedroom waiting for her to stop, feeling there was nothing he could do to help, and also that he was somehow to blame for her distress. Eventually his parents divorced when he was sixteen. At university he felt like an outsider and was anxious all through his early twenties. After a few casual sexual contacts, he met Penny and was drawn to her outgoing personality and sense of fun. He was instantly attracted to her and saw her as the sort of independent woman he could enjoy things with and who would not rely on him for support.

In their sex life they enjoyed some foreplay and mutual touch but were not able to proceed to intercourse due to the pain problem. Penny agreed to try vaginal dilators at home to train her muscles to stretch and expand sufficiently for penetration. At the same time in therapy, we explored her identification with a mother who was pressured into unwanted sex, and how Penny was aware of not wanting to be treated like that. Although James was patient and tolerant, I suggested she was unconsciously identifying with a mother who gave in to sex to appease her husband. Penny had projected her anger at her father on to James and her brain was responding as if she herself was under pressure, which was impairing blood flow and creating an unconscious block to genital arousal (Hiller, 1996). Specifically, although Penny wanted her vaginal passage to expand, her mOFC was not assessing the context as safe and therefore messages from the PAG to the POSC, signalling arousal to proceed, were not being sent. With this integrated approach Penny was able to eventually use the dilators without pain, and the couple were ready to move to increased genital contact with sensate focus exercises.

Although James previously said he had been able to maintain his erection with Penny, he was dismayed to experience loss of erection once there was the possibility of penetration. I suggested that his anxiety about hurting Penny might be causing an increase in cortisol which could be inhibiting his arousal, so that blood flow to the genitals was decreased. We also discussed the role of an unconscious identification with a disappointing and absent father, causing involuntary sexual disempowerment, as a further factor leading to erectile difficulty (Hiller, 1993). From a neurobiological perspective, his mOFC was responding as if the risk of causing distress to his partner was still present, so that penetrative sex became linked to an anxiety-provoking act, similar to how Penny had felt. Messages from his brain to his genitals which would eventually increase nitric oxide and an erectile response, had become impaired. With his increased understanding of the underlying issues, and a careful sensate focus approach, the couple moved from partial insertion to full penetration in a few months, with both partners eventually experiencing pleasure from sex.

CHAPTER 5

Commitment and parenting

W hen two people enter into a committed relationship they generally have hopes for a future together and an awareness of the strong loving feelings they have towards each other. Recently neuroscience has taken us closer to defining the neural correlates of enduring attachment bonds, drawing on the neurobiology of affiliation. Feldman (2017) describes how the enduring attachment bond is the result of biobehavioural synchrony—the coordination of biological and behavioural processes between attachment partners. A critical component of romantic attachments is the regular social contact, which facilitates the development of social synchrony. For this synchrony to take place there is ongoing activation of the neural systems for reward, stress management, and affiliation. In a positive nurturing relationship people will experience each other's company as a combination of enjoyable, calming, reassuring, and bonding. Patterns of behaviour repeated by the partner become familiar, so that reward salience for the new attachment eventually leads to the reorganisation of neural networks. Both oxytocin (OT) and dopamine–oxytocin connectivity are central to the human ability to form long-term attachments, with OT creating calmness and dopamine (DA) adding motivation and vigour to the pair bond. Enduring romantic partnerships in humans combine higher order cortical and subcortical integration, enabling meaningful loving feelings to emerge from associations, experiences, and memory.

Love and commitment may not be a component of the desire to procreate, but for some people it is a starting point for wanting to have children. Becoming parents creates huge changes and challenges, many of which are positive, but a significant proportion of partners who become parents experience a sudden decline in intimacy and relationship satisfaction after the birth of the first child (Doss & Rhoades, 2017). Sleep deprivation, responsibilities of caring for a newborn, and alterations in relationship dynamics notwithstanding, how do neural changes impact on the couple's sexual contact? Research looking at brain activity in reward areas with fMRI scans found that following childbirth, women had increased sexual inhibition and lowered sexual interest, using standard scales, when compared with women who had not given birth. This difference was accounted for by the ventral tegmental area (VTA) in new mothers becoming activated in response to the needs of the baby, along with the release of more oxytocin in response to babies than to sexual themes. However, when intranasal oxytocin was given, both groups of women had increased VTA activation when viewing sexual themes and crying infants (Gregory et al., 2015). On a neurobiological level, decreased sexual desire in new mothers appears to be mediated by the need to bond with the baby through raised oxytocin levels, rather than with the partner, at that early phase of caregiver–infant attachment.

Along with strong attachment there is a marked tendency for the caregiver to experience powerful protective behaviours towards the baby. Turning again to monogamous prairie voles who form mate attachments for rearing offspring, researchers have found that female prairie voles produce short term vasopressin (VP) increases after giving birth, accompanied by hostile behaviour to intruders, when their offspring are under threat from attack. This response is similar to the inter-male aggression shown in male prairie voles, who require VP to perform strong mate-guarding activities after becoming attached to a female following copulation (Carter, 1992; Panksepp, 1998). OT and VP are now thought to both have a significant role in parenting as well as pair-bonding and sexual behaviour, but separating out the role of each neuropeptide is complex. Carter (2017a) discusses how OT and VP bind to each other's receptors, depending on context, and moreover create an OT–VP pathway with dynamic features. This makes studying the contribution of each one to attachment, bonding, safety, and defensiveness particularly problematic for researchers. Although some evidence has been reported on how VP and its receptors influences maternal care, much still remains to be explored (Bayerl & Bosch, 2018).

Men's behaviour and priorities change too after the birth of a child, and this is linked to hormonal changes in new fathers. Testosterone drops by a third and oestrogen increases after a birth, enabling caregiver activities and bonding. Prolactin, associated with lactation in women, rises in new fathers by 20 per cent in the last three weeks of a partner's pregnancy, thereby increasing nurturing behaviours. At the same time men's cortisol levels double, leading to more alertness to the newborn baby. Low testosterone levels also have a role in raising awareness of a baby crying, and interestingly this occurs whether men are fathers or not (Fleming et al., 2002). With lowered testosterone, men tend to experience decreased sex drive in the first few weeks after the birth. Maternal preoccupation with caregiving is stimulated by floods of oxytocin and dopamine, enhanced by breastfeeding and regular skin contact with the infant. This combination creates physical and emotional satisfaction for the mother. Whether desire for sexual contact with her partner decreases or is possibly absent, and when it might return, will depend on the relationship quality.

These hormonal changes, occurring in the early parenting phase, are transient however, and couples tend to resume sexual interactions in a matter of weeks, although the order in which different sexual activities occur sheds an interesting light on couple dynamics. Medical advice is to wait for six weeks before re-engaging sexually, but from an in-depth analysis of 304 women in the first three months post-partum, Hipp et al. (2012) found that 40 per cent of women masturbated before that time period. Performing oral sex was the first partnered activity to resume, with sexual intercourse happening later. Most women reported that the partner's wish for sexual contact was the main factor influencing their level of intimacy after childbirth. Various partner-related factors such as social support and positive involvement in the birth were significant influences on when intercourse, generally male-led, was resumed (Hipp et al., 2012). It is possible too that prolactin in men has a role in the early weeks after the baby arrives, due to the negative feedback loop this hormone has with DA. Prolactin enhances the secretion of DA, but DA restrains prolactin release. As the father's prolactin production decreases, testosterone, and DA, return to normal levels, with the result that sexual desire can return too. Male desire for sexual contact seems to be the driving force impacting women's wish for couple activity post-partum, although new mothers do have individual desire, as shown by the level of masturbation reported in the study.

We know from fMRI studies involving mothers viewing their own child compared with another known infant, that the increases in DA and noradrenaline release are similar to those found when partners view photos of a lover while in the scanner. Maternal love, however, does not activate the posterior hypothalamus and the hippocampus, both of which are part of neural changes in romantic love (Bartels & Zeki, 2004). So, while maternal and romantic love do have some common neural correlates, there are distinct and crucial differences on the level of brain activity.

Summary and clinical relevance

Requests for therapy in the early months after childbirth occur less frequently than later, when couples have been together for longer. Some couples do experience a setback while adapting to a baby and struggle to regain confidence in their sexual contact. Hormonal changes, altered sleep patterns, and changes in partner attention can cause frustrations which become embedded in hostile communication patterns. In new mothers, the brain systems involved in oxytocin release and bonding become directed towards the baby rather than towards the partner, which can be seen as a necessary evolutionary role, and is usually a temporary one. However, this phase is not always short, and understanding the underlying neurobiology can provide confidence for the therapist. An explanation to the couple could help to alleviate misunderstandings when partners find it difficult to regain intimacy during this sensitive phase.

Robert and Helen

Robert and Helen, both thirty, had lived together for five years and were in crisis when they started couple therapy. They described regular bickering and rows following the birth of their first baby, who was then eight months old, and the absence of sex, which was upsetting for

Robert. Helen complained that Robert was unable to cope with their son's needs, while Robert said he couldn't remember the feeding and changing routines. Helen wanted everything done a certain way, but she became very angry if he asked her what to do next with the baby. Robert felt he was constantly criticised and getting things wrong, however much he tried. Helen accused him of being immature and of not managing to have an equal relationship, as they had discussed before the baby was born. Both partners were devoted to the baby, but Robert was under pressure to reach targets at work and found the requirements of being a father and employee too demanding. Helen desperately wanted to be nurturing, as she could not recall hands-on care from her own mother, but at the same time needed a break from childcare occasionally. Robert also wanted to be different from his emotionally unavailable father, both with his son and with Helen. His mother was described as a quiet, kind, and caring person with a small circle of friends. Robert had hoped that his sex life with Helen would resume again, as this helped him to feel wanted rather than always in trouble. Helen was completely uninterested in sex, saying she was too resentful of how much she was expected to do with the baby and in the home. They both agreed that sex had worked well before the baby came along.

Helen grew up in Scotland and had very few friends in London. She described her mother as over emotional, without self-awareness, and someone who couldn't be reasoned with. Her father buried himself in work and drank too much. She was glad to get away from home and move to London when she met Robert. His inability to grasp the domestic and childcare routines was infuriating her and she wanted them to talk about how to share tasks, but he insisted on leaving the room rather than discussing the issues. Robert found the only way to cope with Helen's criticisms was to go away until he could calm himself and think clearly. He found Helen's tone prevented him from grasping what she was saying because he felt attacked by her sharp manner. For her part, Helen called Robert inactive and useless. On an unconscious level Helen and Robert both appeared to expect the other to compensate for the lack of sensitive care from their same-sex parents. The arrival of a baby disrupted the balance of their communications, resulting in disappointment and accusations from Helen, and confusion from Robert, who became avoidant.

In therapy we explored projections from their upbringing, and how the couple were addressing the current childcare needs. It emerged that Helen was so anxious about getting everything right that she had not left the baby with Robert, to give him time to get used to his son, for more than a few minutes. Describing the development of biobehavioural synchrony, linked with Helen's trust issues, was very helpful to the couple. They responded to discussions about the importance of regular physical and emotional contact, facilitating OT and DA release, for caregivers to connect with and learn how to manage a baby. It was agreed that Robert's mother, who they both had confidence in, could initially watch Robert and the baby until he understood how to look after him through experience instead of instructions only. This would give Helen time to go to the gym or meet a friend, and reduce her irritation, which was preventing oxytocin and opioid release when she was with Robert. Helen was encouraged to discuss plans calmly with Robert so he could take in what was expected and to make notes if that helped him. On a physical level the couple agreed to hug in bed, with no expectations until the atmosphere at home was calmer. Although it took a while for the resentments and arguments to recede, the couple found a more productive way to communicate and were then able to gradually resume sexual activity.

CHAPTER 6

Infidelity

Debates abound on whether humans are naturally monogamous or non-monogamous, and one suggestion is that we have evolved to seek and prefer social monogamy without necessarily managing sexual monogamy (de Boer et al., 2012). Social monogamy includes loving relationships, selective attachments, long-term bonds, family groups, and wariness or aggression to strangers. Issues around infidelity raise significant cultural, personal, and moral questions. Terms such as extra-dyadic sex and extra-pair mating are used in research, where infidelity is defined as including any physical sexual activity with an individual other than one's current, self-identified committed relationship partner. Expectations of fidelity are strong in our society, and infidelity causes immense distress for everyone involved. Dissatisfaction with the primary relationship, attachment style, and opportunity are among the key factors explored to account for infidelity, and self-regulation and commitment to the pair bond are also a focus of research. Neuroscience has added to the infidelity topic, drawing on genetic, fMRI studies, and animal models to identify the possible genetic and biological mechanisms associated with sex outside the committed partnership. It seems that pursuing the goal of romantic and sexual reward can be more powerful than the fear of destabilisation when someone becomes very attracted to a new person. If this strong attraction does occur, dopamine (DA) and noradrenaline (NA) will flood the brain's reward and pleasure centres, creating heightened excitement, while the prefrontal cortex and amygdala become blocked. With a loss of both critical thinking and self-awareness, people are more likely to become irrational and take risks that are out of character (Treas & Giesen, 2000).

Despite the societal norm, the assumption of sexual exclusivity, and general disapproval if this is not adhered to, infidelity occurs quite frequently, suggesting that many people can maintain close relationships with more than one person simultaneously. Data on numbers of people engaging in sex outside the committed partnership has consistently shown higher numbers for men than for women, but the ratio varies somewhat according to age, and to the decade when surveys were undertaken. Below the age of thirty the numbers are similar, but from then on men are more likely than women to admit to infidelity, with a widening gap from the age of forty (Wang, 2018). Estimates of infidelity among married heterosexual people vary from 22 to 29 per cent for men and 10 to 17 per cent for women, but among unmarried couples the rates rise to 57 per cent and 54 per cent for men and women, respectively. Among the gay population, over 50 per cent of gay men report having sex outside their committed relationship. In light of the description in Chapter 5 of the strong links between the amygdala and the hypothalamus in male brains, this finding is unsurprising. Moreover, this is backed up by a neuroimaging meta-analyses study confirming gender differences in sexual behaviour, based on how the brain receives and sends information to the rest of the body (Peoppl et al., 2016)

Can neuroscience offer an explanation as to why some people are content with sexual exclusivity while others experience strong attraction to someone else? Fisher's work (1998, 2004), discussed above, described the three brain systems underpinning human reproductive strategy: lust, or sex drive (dependent on oestrogen and testosterone), which evolved to motivate sexual behaviour in general; romantic attraction (dependent on DA, noradrenaline, and serotonin) which focuses mating energy on a specific selected partner, and attachment (dependent on oxytocin and vasopressin). Although these three basic neural systems interact with one another and many other brain systems, they can impact separately on emotions, making it biologically possible to express deep feelings of attachment for one partner, while feeling intense romantic love for another individual, while also feeling a sex drive for even more extra-dyadic partners (Tsapelas et al., 2010).

Many genetic studies have examined the brain's DA reward pathway. Acevedo et al. (2012) found that activity in the ventral tegmental area (where DA originates) was associated with long-term romantic love, specifically the dopamine receptors, which come in different forms. Investigations have highlighted the dopamine D4 receptor gene (DRD4) which varies considerably within populations, and has a specific form, or allele, the 7-repeat (7R) allele. This genetic variant has been associated with increased sensitivity to adverse experiences, which can result in issues with many areas of emotional expression, including behavioural problems in children and aggression, gambling, and addiction in adults. ADHD (attention deficit hyperactivity disorder) and decreased attention are among the behaviours that have a well-established link with the 7-repeat allele of DRD4 (King et al., 2016), and there is also a well-documented association between the 7R allele and the prediction of disorganised attachment at three years of age, when combined with low birthweight and maternal caregiving styles (Wazana, 2016).

Uncommitted and risky sexual behaviours have similarly been linked to genes coding for motivation and reward in the brain. Garcia et al. (2010) collected sexual history data from young adults and genotyped them to measure the 7-repeat allele of the D4 receptor, to explore the genetic basis of infidelity. They found that individuals carrying 7R were significantly more likely to have engaged in one-night stands as well as infidelity. By contrast, those without this genotype were more likely to be monogamous and not engage in uncommitted sexual behaviours. Although these results provide a link between people with the genetic variation of the 7R allele on the D4 receptor and casual sex, the researchers point out that the behavioural outcomes of monogamy contrasted with uncommitted sexual behaviour are probabilistic, so describing the genotype as a "promiscuity gene" would be false. Notwithstanding a link between genetic coding for risky sexual behaviour and infidelity, it is well understood that alcohol intake impairs the ability of the prefrontal cortex to inhibit actions that are potentially damaging (Abernathy et al., 2010), an effect that would undermine decision–making about sex outside the committed relationship. As with all behaviours, environmental factors, including opportunity, are crucial for genetic influences to be expressed.

Specific variants of the receptor genes for oxytocin (OT) and vasopressin (VP) have also been researched extensively in animal studies. When prairie voles copulate, OT is released in the nucleus accumbens brain area in females, but vasopressin release occurs in the ventral pallidum in males. This combination facilitates DA circulation, motivates attachment behaviours, and is vital for selection of a mating partner for life (Carter, 1992; Young & Wang, 2004). Moreover, sexual fidelity among prairie voles has been clearly linked to a polymorphism (more than one allele) of a vasopressin gene, coding for a specific receptor, the V1a VP receptor (Lim & Young, 2004; Ophir et al., 2008).

How useful is the research on monogamous voles, and can cross species comparisons be made to enhance our understanding of human sexuality and infidelity? Neuroscience has confirmed the validity of comparing certain aspects of vole and human mating. In a neuroimaging study of couples in loving committed relationships, Acevedo et al. (2012) found that the length of time couples had been together was related to increased activity in the ventral pallidum, the brain region from which male prairie voles release VP, among other neural regions. One of these is the globus pallidus, which has also been demonstrated as vital for pair-bonding in prairie voles. Leknes and Tracey (2008) studied motivated behavioural responses in humans and confirmed the role of the nucleus accumbens and ventral pallidum for neural processing of pleasure, and a review of the data by Smith et al. (2009) described the ventral pallidum as a limbic final common pathway for sexual reward, as well as food and drug rewards. Moreover, intranasal OT has been shown to reduce both negative communications and cortisol levels, compared to a placebo, during conflictual couple discussions (Ditzen et al., 2009). Recall also that during sexual arousal and orgasm circulating OT levels increased significantly in women, while men release VP during arousal and then OT with orgasm (Carmichael et al., 1987; Murphy et al., 1987).

Empirical research to explore the genetics of infidelity has examined the link between human pair-bonding and genes coding for OT and VP receptors, but with somewhat equivocal results to date. Questioning a large British sample of female twins on sexual behaviour, Cherkas et al. (2005) found that genetic influences accounted for 41 per cent of the variation on infidelity and 38 per cent of the variation on lifetime sexual partners, with a strong correlation between the two traits, but their group showed no impact of the VP receptor V1a on these aspects of women's sexual behaviour. Walum et al. (2008) directly examined the link between pair-bonding patterns in the male partners of couples and genes coding for the VP receptor V1a, and a different outcome emerged for the genetic coding. More than 500 couples were assessed in depth for relationship quality and couple problems. Human and prairie vole gene sequences for receptor V1a are not homologous, that is, they do not have the same sequencing of alleles. However, humans do have three polymorphic alleles (334) in a corresponding region of the VP system. Researchers in the Walum et al. study used various measures of a dynamic assessment scale, and also devised a Partner Bonding Scale to measure the level of attachment between partners. Although the study was not a direct measure of infidelity, the results suggested that men carrying more than one 334 allele scored lower on partner satisfaction and couple bonding and were twice as likely to have experienced a relationship crisis in the previous year.

A later study by the same team on a large sample of men and women in romantic relationships used the Partner Bonding Scale again, along with other measures, to assess the link between twelve variants of the OT receptor gene and pair-bonding related behaviour (Walum et al., 2012). Subjects were female twin pairs and their partners, and results showed that out of the twelve OT variants tested, just one specific allele of the OT receptor gene emerged as significantly associated with pair-bonding behaviours in women, but not in men. Contrasting results were found yet again by Zietsch et al. (2015) who analysed extra-pair mating in more than 7000 Finnish twins and their siblings, and also tested extra-pair mating for links with OT and VP receptor genes. This team found no association in either sex for the OT genes, but did find an association, in women only, between five variations of the V1a gene and infidelity. An expected outcome would have been a link between V1a and male infidelity, but this was not the case. Perhaps this is explained by the different measures used in the various studies: Walum et al. (2008, 2012) questioned couples about relationship problems, bonding, and partner satisfaction, whereas Zietsch et al. (2015) asked subjects about sexual behaviour outside the committed pair bond—a different measure albeit an allied one. Similar to the Cherkas et al. (2005) study, however, Zietsch et al. (2015) found that genes contributed to 40 per cent of the variation in women's extra-pair mating and 62 per cent in men's.

Other factors apart from genes are relevant to all human traits, and how genes impact on behaviour across the life course will depend to a considerable degree on the epigenome—the chemical marks that influence whether or not the gene is expressed. Childhood experiences rearrange the epigenome, and the study of environmental factors that contribute to the release of information carried by genes is known as epigenetics. This emerging area of scientific research has increased our understanding of certain diseases, but such is the difficulty of replicating research into gene associations for complex behavioural traits that many reports are considered misleading and should be read with caution (Hewitt, 2012). Thus, while all these results do seem to confirm a genetic predisposition for infidelity, the role and specific form of DA, OT, and VP receptors associated with extra-pair mating still remains unclear. On a positive note, science has revealed that epigenetic changes are reversible over time, confirming the value of therapeutic work in this painful area of relationship management.

Summary and clinical relevance

Couples struggling with infidelity generally present with significant emotional hurt, abandonment fears, and anger issues. Some people decide that staying with a partner is too difficult when they experience betrayal, while others work hard to tolerate and accept what has occurred. Understanding the different neural correlates underpinning lust, attraction, and attachment can be part of the healing process in some cases, when the hurt person is able to accept they are loved even though their partner has been involved with someone else. In therapy a balance is required between expressions of hostility towards the acting-out partner, and the containment of views that could further harm a fragile relationship. Although genetic factors have been found to contribute to sex outside the committed partnership, ascribing acts of infidelity to inherited neural pathways is unlikely to be productive for healing in the relationship. Crucially humans, unlike other mammals, are capable of exercising prefrontal cortex decision-making abilities to make choices about behaviours, including sexual acts, despite the power of primitive subcortical urges, developmental experiences, and the longing for emotional and physical connections. At times though, the combination of unmet needs and desire is strong, and finding another sexual partner presents a solution, albeit a temporary one. With a new partner, DA and OT release are high, creating motivation, excitement, and arousal. Genetic predisposition may well play a part, but highlighting individual responsibility in the context of couple dynamics is one of the central features when working with infidelity. Awareness by clinicians of the genetic evidence could increase understanding of the difficulty experienced by the acting-out partner, while at the same time managing intense emotional expression during couple sessions.

Case vignettes

Chris and Kelly

Chris and Kelly were in their late fifties and had been married for three years when Kelly discovered text messages on Chris's phone, indicating he was involved with another woman. She was very shocked and confronted Chris at once. Both partners had been married unhappily before and each had an adult child from their previous marriage, who lived in their own homes. Kelly and Chris had met through an online dating site and thought they were well matched, and very fortunate at that stage in their lives to have the chance of a good relationship. Kelly knew that Chris had had quite a few sexual partners after his divorce, while she had been more cautious. Part of Kelly's distress was because their sex life was enjoyable and remained active, contributing to her hurt and fury that Chris had sought a sexual outlet elsewhere. He was a businessman who travelled for work, and he admitted to meeting up with one of the other women he had dated while searching for a partner online. She had been very disappointed when he chose Kelly and not her, and later contacted him again about meeting. He was unable to resist and was drawn to the excitement. In Chris's background, his father, whom he was close to, was a womaniser whose affairs caused his mother immense distress. He recalled regular heated arguments between his parents as a child, when his mother shouted a lot, and he would lie in bed wishing she would stop. Although he was upset at the thought of causing pain to Kelly, he convinced himself it would not matter, saying the other woman was fun but unimportant. I suggested this was a coping mechanism from childhood when Chris wanted to believe the other women in his father's life posed no threat and his parents would not divorce. When confronted with the infidelity he was clear that he wished to stay with Kelly, and he immediately ended the other relationship.

Kelly came from a family who had struggled financially, due to her parents' job problems. She was exposed to her mother's anger with her father, who had a gambling habit which he lied about, and which caused many days off work. She was determined to earn her own money and not live with a man who deceived her. Chris had a very different background, having inherited from his parents and then becoming successful in his own right. Kelly saw him as an ambitious and strong man who she felt safe with, despite Chris having told her about his father's infidelities. It is possible that Kelly had an unconscious desire to reform a man who was at risk of deceiving her, in order to gain control, in a way her mother was unable to do with her father. For Kelly the infidelity was a profound betrayal. Chris struggled to understand her reactions because he insisted she was the one he loved, and he wanted to stay with her. They continued to have regular sexual intercourse throughout therapy, which reassured them both about the strength of their relationship. Describing the different brain systems underpinning the sex drive, attraction, and attachment was helpful to the couple, although painful for Kelly. However, she was able to accept the possibility of loving one person and remaining attached to them while at the same time experiencing attraction to another. As a couple they could also see that Chris's sex drive was strong, and he would need to change his approach to sexual urges if he wanted Kelly to trust him.

While addressing different ways of relating that could bring more emotional closeness, we also focused on how Chris was repeating the pattern of his father's infidelity, which on a conscious level he had no wish to do. We talked about how Chris could be making choices for himself and for Kelly to avoid the impact of another betrayal, which Kelly said would definitely lead to divorce. Chris desperately did not want to lose Kelly and was keen to hear about the ability of prefrontal cortex reasoning to overcome emotions, such as feeling attracted to another person. Discussions of the difference between conscious awareness and planning, compared to primitive sexual drives, were helpful to Chris. Kelly remained unsettled for some time and wanted to know how she could trust Chris not to be drawn to further infidelities. Time was spent in sessions finding ways that Chris could reassure Kelly that he was always where he said he would be, especially when away from home. Despite uncertainties that kept arising, therapy helped both partners to understand what had happened and how they could maintain their couple bond.

Gina and Paula

Gina and Paula met at medical school and were both qualified doctors in their twenties when they came to see me. Paula discovered evidence online that Gina had become involved with another doctor in the hospital where she was completing her training and was devastated by the threat to their relationship. Both women came from families with divorced parents, and very much hoped they could stay together long term. Paula's mother had ended her marriage when she realised she was gay in her mid-fifties and went to live with her female partner, and her father went to live abroad, much to Paula's dismay. Gina's father left the family for a work colleague, and Gina's mother then started another relationship. In couple sessions Gina was full of remorse but reluctant to give any details about what had happened between her and her colleague. She did admit that the colleague had pursued her, making her feel attractive and wanted. However, she denied intimate sexual contact, although Paula had found email messages that appeared to suggest the contrary. Paula felt very betrayed, insecure, and hurt.

Deconstructing the events leading up to Paula's discovery of the emails proved painful for both women, and they became very distressed. It emerged that Paula had struggled with studying medicine and was unsure about her decision to become a GP. Gina had supported her through the training and encouraged her to continue with her practice placement, while she herself was enjoying the demands of working on a hospital ward, despite the heavy workload. Gina admitted that Paula's dissatisfaction with work was putting a strain on the relationship: she felt more like a work coach or counsellor at times, and really missed the early days when they had first met. At that stage they had discussed having children and who would try to get pregnant first. However, Paula had begun to complain a lot and Gina felt the fun had disappeared. Uncovering this caused additional pain for Paula, who felt somehow blamed for what had happened. Gina requested an individual session, and it was agreed that Paula would also have one. Gina revealed that the other person was a consultant whom she admired, and that the attraction was very flattering, although she did not want to be with the other woman and to repeat what her father had done to her mother. Gina was surprised and puzzled by her emotions, but discussing the three discrete but connected brain systems underpinning lust, attraction, and attachment helped her to make sense of her confusion. She seemed to have chosen a vulnerable partner in Paula, who she loved and who needed her. Entertaining the idea of casual sex posed a challenge for her to overcome. She wanted to stay with Paula, taking on board her uncertainties and need for care. To help Gina resist the temptation we discussed the balance between rational thinking in the prefrontal cortex, and emotional states connected to developmental experiences, emanating from subcortical brain systems.

In Paula's session she began to explore her abandonment fears, and to see she demanded too much from Gina, perhaps as an unconscious test of loyalty, which her parents had failed to manage. She was relieved to know that Gina could love her and be strongly attached to her while being attracted to someone else, even though the concept was distressing and left her insecure. Paula decided to pursue her own individual therapy to relieve the strain on the relationship. We continued to focus on trust issues in the couple work, remembering why they were together and finding ways to bring back shared activities and lightness into their relationship, which they both very much wished to continue.

CHAPTER 7

Breaking up and rejection

C onnecting intimately to a partner brings with it the many pleasures of loving, knowing, and being known by another person, but also the various risks; perhaps the main risk being the relationship ending through rejection. Breaking up due to romantic rejection is a particular form of loss and psychological pain that includes a powerful sense of despair and deprivation, the frustration of a need to love and be loved, and a wish to maintain meaningful social relationships. After a break-up it is quite common for the rejected person to still feel strong positive feelings for the rejector and to attempt to regain the relationship. Distress following a break-up is often referred to as having a broken heart, as if the impact was physical, and indeed various studies have found an overlap between the brain responses to physical pain and the hurt experienced with relationship endings, including significant social loss. Neuroimaging studies have highlighted the neural regions and neurochemical substrates that were similar, and those that differentiated psychological from physical pain (Eisenberger, 2015; Kross et al., 2011; Meerwijk et al., 2012). Being able to distinguish between these is necessary to ensure that physical pain draws attention to bodily needs whereas emotional/psychological pain motivates people towards social and relationship goals (Ferris et al., 2019).

We might expect that being rejected or being accepted would be linked to different brain events, but on the level of neurobiology this is not quite the case. Interesting similarities have emerged when comparing the brain activation of individuals after a painful break-up with those in secure relationships. One system, the endogenous opioid system (whereby opioids are released by neural activation rather than being taking in through an exogenous, or external route) plays a crucial role in both maintaining homeostasis and in alleviating pain signals. This system provides the neural substrate for social distress and social attachments by producing beta-endorphins. These are endogenous opioid neuropeptides which bind to a mu-opioid receptor (MOR) and serve to reduce pain sensations. Endorphins are also hormones that create feelings of pleasure, such as with love and during orgasm, and at other times, for example, with exercise, they can produce a surge of positive sensations. Because MORs are found throughout the brain and body, beta-endorphins can regulate a range of systems to have their effect, depending on the location of the receptors.

Using PET scans in a laboratory study into changes in neuronal pathways, Hsu et al. (2013) found measurable changes in MOR activation during both social rejection and, rather surprisingly, during acceptance/positive social experiences. However, the responses differed in strength and created different outcomes. When mu-opioids are released two brain areas are triggered: the amygdala which assesses the strength of the emotion, and the pregenual cingulate cortex to which it is connected, the region controlling changes in mood based on the event. Mu-opioid receptor activation was greater during social rejection and was similar to the response with physical pain, while acceptance/being liked, resulted in weaker activation of this system. Moreover, subjects who suffered less with psychological pain, so were assumed to be higher in what was termed "trait resiliency", produced higher levels of activation in specific brain regions (the amygdala, periaqueductal grey and anterior cingulate cortex) suggesting a protective role for opioid release in these areas.

Studies using fMRI scans to measure neural response patterns associated with attachment and the distress of rejection have also confirmed an overlap in the activity of certain brain regions, which helps to explain some of the features people experience following a break-up.

Both Fisher et al. (2010) and Hsu et al. (2020) compared groups of rejected and romantically accepted individuals and discovered extensive anatomical overlap between the two conditions. Prefrontal cortex activation when rejected was significant in subjects from both the above studies, indicating the particular importance of executive function—the ability to self-regulate and plan—when suffering the psychological pain of a rejection. We need executive function at this time because reacting to a serious loss requires the management of conflicting thoughts, evaluation of the outcome of actions, and suppression of behaviours that could be damaging; all part of judgement and decision-making about how to cope with an ending. Executive function is achieved through extensive connections between the ventromedial prefrontal cortex and the VTA, amygdala, cingulate gyrus, thalamus, and other brain regions associated with personal and social decision-making. The two fMRI studies described above demonstrate that activation of reward and survival areas, shown by the ventral tegmental area changes and the extended forebrain gain/loss system, are present not only in early-stage romantic passion but also when a relationship has ended unhappily, and the person who has been left still has strong feelings for the rejector. This is an emotionally confused and chaotic state, occurring when these brain regions trigger a rejection reaction, especially if this includes the urge or goal to win the ex-mate back. Activation of the reward/survival system can be seen as an evolutionarily adaptive response, albeit one that risks further pain if the goal is not achieved, and the break-up is final. At the same time reward/survival brain activation can lead distressed individuals to seek social support from someone who they trust.

Research has shown what happens in the brain when people are comforted by holding the hand of a loved one, or even just looking at their picture. Physical touch with handholding, or emotional arousal from visual imagery, causes a decrease in pain-related neurological responses in the cingulate gyrus (part of the cingulate cortex) and anterior insula, and a decrease in reported pain (Eisenberger, 2015). Increased activation in the cingulate gyrus and anterior insula, described above in the Fisher et al. (2010) and Hsu et al. (2020) research, respectively, shares the function of co-ordinating responses to internal and external events, and provides the neural basis for integrating affect, cognition, and behaviour based on conscious awareness. Cingulate gyrus and anterior insula activation is considered to have a critical role in creating subjective feelings, which then become integrated and form the basis of conscious experiences (Medford & Critchley, 2010). Conscious appraisal of our feelings matters at all times, but perhaps especially so with relationship endings, when people are likely to experience self-doubt along with emotional pain and, at times, despair. Triggering the reward/survival mechanism leads to a search for meaningful connections with others to provide a sense of self-worth and may underpin the obsessive nature of behaviour when someone is first rejected (Fisher et al., 2010). This mechanism is also likely to account for the distraught and desperate feelings experienced by many people after a break-up. Appealing to the rejector as a way of finding comfort and hopefully to continue the relationship would be a high-risk strategy, involving the possibility of further rejection and distress. We can see though that turning to significant others is adaptive and reassuring. Psychotherapy has a role here in providing an enriching environment for emotional and cognitive processing, which enhances conscious awareness. According to Cozolino (2017, p. 399) constructing a narrative in the therapeutic process "allows us to combine—in conscious memory—our knowledge, sensations, feelings and behaviours in a coherent manner that supports neural network integration".

Breaking up and significant social loss are often accompanied by feelings of depression. Both PET scans and fMRI studies of depressed subjects indicate abnormalities of cerebral blood flow to the amygdala, thalamus, anterior cingulate cortex, and prefrontal cortex. With depressive symptoms, impairment of oxytocin and vasopressin release, decreased serotonin in the midbrain and amygdala, and elevated cortisol levels have also been shown (Kaltenboeck & Harmer, 2018). Moreover, a decrease in dopamine release from the ventral tegmental area (VTA), possibly in connection with lowered oxytocin, has been found to accompany depressive symptoms, so motivation and pleasure in life will be reduced. If depression reaches clinical levels, antidepressants such as SSRIs (selective serotonin reuptake inhibitors) could be recommended. Medications such as sertraline, escitalopram, and fluoxetine are commonly prescribed SSRIs, designed to prevent serotonin uptake, or reabsorption, thereby increasing the serotonin available in the brain to carry signals between neurons. If more of this transmitter is available to carry chemical messengers, it can regulate feelings and help to increase mood, according to the theories. However, managing emotional pain and depression following a relationship ending, or for any other reason, does not have to be an either/or approach in terms of treatment. Antidepressant medication aims to increase the available serotonin and reduce negative emotions, which facilitates the brain's ability to rewire. By altering the neurotransmitter balance, the effectiveness of therapy approaches to change unwanted behaviours and relationship patterns can be enhanced (Cozolino, 2017).

Can neuroscience help us to understand why some people feel distress but are able to accept a break-up, while others suffer very badly for a considerable time? Yet another group will exert efforts to restart the relationship even if it was an unsatisfactory one. Sensitivity to rejection is greater in some people than others, and this is possibly because they release lower levels of opioids when hurt by an ending, indicating a decreased ability to protect themselves. Research suggests that following romantic rejection (and serious social loss) an initial painful low opioid state has the function of motivating the distressed person to improve their emotional condition by turning to others for comfort, although this might include trying to connect with the rejector in the hope of reducing the pain. Seeking positive social contacts is a highly adaptive response because it will then lead to endogenous opioid release, rebalancing the emotional system and reducing the sense of loss (Tchalova & Eisenberger, 2015). Neuroimaging studies reveal that individuals who report higher daily levels of social support, and those who spent more time with friends during adolescence, have reduced activation of the anterior cingulate cortex and anterior insula in response to social exclusion. Supportive and reassuring contact with others throughout life appears to offer some protection against a more extreme sense of loss, on the level of brain responses and therefore feelings, when a romantic relationship is over.

Based on the premise that the MOR system has a dual role in both reducing social distress and mediating social reward, Meier et al. (2021) have described a mu-opioid feedback model of social behaviour linking stressful developmental experiences to the ability to modulate pain. According to the mu-opioid feedback model, positive social experiences during development lead to endogenous mu-opioid release in reward and motivation brain areas and thereby increase anticipation and seeking out of satisfying social interactions

BRAIN RESPONSE   EMOTIONAL/BEHAVIOURAL RESPONSE

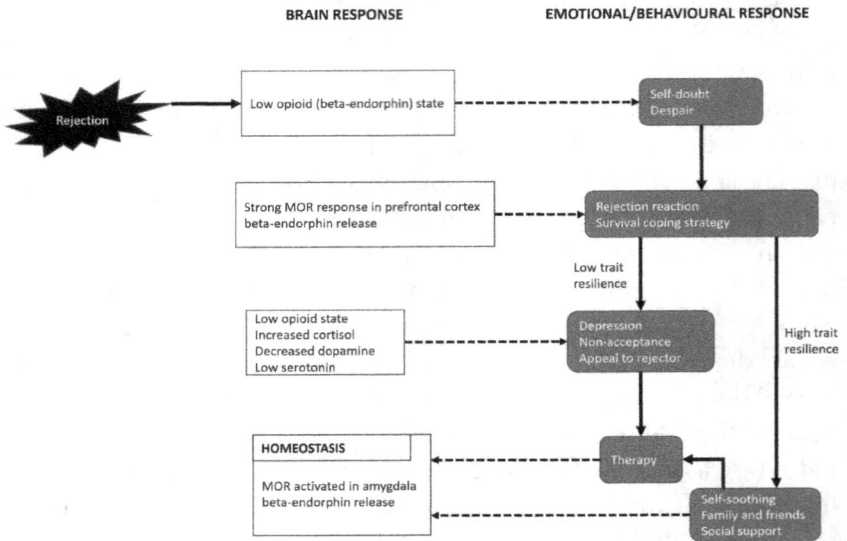

Figure 3 Diagram illustrating endogenous opioid system to regain homeostasis after a break-up/rejection

An initial low opioid state accompanied by distress leads to PFC (prefrontal cortex) activation and a strong mu-opioid receptor response, to underpin a coping strategy. Endorphin release facilitates choices about the next step, to find comfort and rebalance emotions, and the pathway at this stage depends on individual resilience. If non-acceptance of the break-up takes place (low trait resilience) the person can seek comfort from friends but might turn to the rejector to continue the relationship, so remain in a low opioid, unhappy state if rejected again. Someone with stronger coping mechanisms, that is, higher trait resilience, is thought to have greater MOR activation in the amygdala, anterior cingulate cortex, and periaqueductal grey, so is more likely to self-soothe, and could also turn to a social support network. Family and friends as well as therapy can all play a vital part in calming the amygdala, through mu-opioid receptor activation and endorphin release, with the aim of eventually regaining emotional homeostasis.

(affiliative loop). Strong social bonds can be formed which decrease sensitivity to both stress and negative, rejecting social cues. In this situation MOR activation increases in pain processing areas and has a protective role. However, repeated negative experiences during childhood are postulated to lead to chronic dysregulation of the mu-opioid system, resulting in hypersensitivity to abandonment and decreased ability to recognise and respond to positive social experiences. This is caused by frequent traumatic interactions which can alter the neurochemistry of the MOR system to a purely protective function (protective loop). An individual who anticipates threat and rejection is more likely to have an insecure attachment style, to struggle to form rewarding long-term relationships, and possibly to suffer a more extreme reaction and greater pain for a longer period following a relationship ending.

Summary and clinical relevance

Painful endings have many similarities to physical pain sensations, which helps to explain how the risk of repeating the experience can lead to avoidance of seeking another relationship. Anger, despair, depression, and stress after the blow of rejection or a break-up—similar to grief reactions—are frequently reported. Strong emotions of significant hurt and loss are common, although they do eventually fade. For some individuals, however, overcoming the intense disappointment of losing a love object can take a long time. Neuroscience has highlighted the role of the mu-opioid receptor in regulating the response to social rejection through the release of endogenous endorphins and has shown how developmental experiences impact the activation of this system. Research has linked early life experiences to the protective role of opioid release in response to endings. This offers an explanation as to why some people are more susceptible to severe distress or might stay in a relationship when they realise the situation is unrewarding. Developmental factors which dysregulate the MOR system can mean that anticipation of the extent of the emotional pain can lead to someone choosing to remain with a partner even when they are unhappy. The emotional upheaval of a break-up can feel like the experience of abandonment. Therapy in this context has a valuable role in providing the psychological equivalent of handholding. Offering emotional support and understanding can be part of a process to trigger endogenous opioid release, re-sculpt neural pathways, and reduce the pain of loss, while also processing the meaning of the unsatisfactory relationship with the aim of avoiding a similar situation in the future.

Case vignette

Denise

Denise, who I described in Chapter 2, contacted me a few months after the end of couple therapy because Warren had decided the relationship was over. He refused to comply with her wish for a baby, and eventually said he couldn't manage her blaming emotional attacks. Even though he still cared for her, he found her anger became too much to cope with. Denise admitted that regulating her outbursts of resentment had been very difficult. She was distraught at being on her own again, having invested so much in Waren and his family, and the prospect of finding another partner was very anxiety provoking. At times she felt frozen and was unable to face the day. Her GP had signed Denise off work for a month due to her problem with concentrating. There was no one in her family to offer support. Her sister wasn't speaking to her, and her parents were emotionally unavailable, although they were begrudgingly letting her temporarily live with them until she found somewhere else. Denise thought her friends were tired of listening to her complaints about Warren. Keeping friendships going had always been a struggle for Denise. She was too embarrassed to bring friends to her house when she was young as the atmosphere was so miserable and her parents were disapproving. At school she remained an outsider, thinking she was different in comparison to the other girls who came from warm environments.

We spent time in individual sessions talking about the brain's mu-opioid response system and how she could gain comfort elsewhere rather than appealing to Warren, who was likely to reject her again. Denise made an effort to contact friends she had lost touch with and to take an interest in their lives, and she tried yoga classes. Nevertheless, Denise continually questioned whether she should ask Warren to resume the relationship on the basis that she would give up the prospect of having her own child. This dilemma was a repetitive theme for months, as she alternated between berating herself for letting Warren go by asking for a baby, and accepting the relationship was not good for her, as they did not want the same things. If she did occasionally meet another man, the comparison with Warren was stark and she was unable to progress the contact. Her repetition of the dilemma she faced seemed to be a desperate search for empathic attention from parents who were too depressed and inattentive to give her the love and warmth she needed so badly. My role was to understand her pain but, and at the same time, to suggest how she could find a way forward. Seeing friends (without expecting ongoing emotional support), taking up sports and exercise, and trying to absorb herself in any distracting activity were part of the healing process. When Denise did eventually decide, spontaneously, to call Warren, his coldness exacerbated her sense of abandonment and took the healing process back a few steps. It took almost a year for her obsessional thoughts about the end of the relationship to decrease to the point when she regained enough confidence to contemplate starting to look for another relationship.

CHAPTER 8

Long-term relationships: staying together unhappily

Couple relationships can last for many years without being rewarding and loving. For some people staying together is preferable to separating, despite an unhappy and unsatisfactory relationship for one or both partners. Neuroscientific investigations have demonstrated how the brain states underpinning negative emotions can cause a further decrease in intimacy between people. Stress for example, alters reactivity in many neural regions involved with attachment and emotional processing, including the hypothalamus, anterior insula, amygdala, anterior cingulate cortex, and ventral striatum (van Oort et al., 2017). If oxytocin (OT) is released this helps to decrease stress by reducing cortisol, the stress hormone, but couples who are disengaged and dissatisfied are unlikely to have interactions such as caring communications and psychological support that stimulate OT release, and they are also more prone to disagreements and arguments. In a laboratory study of couples in a standard instructed couple conflict discussion, Ditzen et al. (2009) compared intranasal OT administration with a placebo. They found that following the conflict, salivary cortisol was significantly reduced in the group who received OT. Moreover, positive communication was increased in the OT group compared with the placebo group during the conflictual discussion. When people live together in an atmosphere of tension and strain, lacking interactions that facilitate warmth and positive emotions, central OT will be unavailable to reduce stress responses and decrease blood pressure. Researchers suggest that OT plays a part not only in the initial building of attachments by decreasing anxiety, possibly by calming amygdala responses, but it also has a role in managing raised emotions in the later stages of relationships (Marazziti et al., 2006). Touch is well documented as facilitating OT release, and Uvnas-Moberg and Peterson (2005) have also described how psychological mechanisms involving empathy and support can stimulate oxytocin and facilitate emotional and physical healing. Paradoxically, oxytocin can also be a response to stress when it can lead people to seek out supportive contact. As previously mentioned, Taylor (2006) demonstrated a "tend and befriend" model of oxytocin release, with research showing how this neuropeptide regulates stress under negative conditions and can underpin peaceful friendly behaviour when situations are problematic.

Frustration and anger are common features of troubled relationships, and there is a substantial literature on the neural substrates of such intense emotions. Experiencing anger activates the basic threat systems; the amygdala, hypothalamus, and periaqueductal grey (Blair, 2012). Of particular relevance to couple relationships are the findings that anger has a motivational orientation towards approach behaviour. This implies that angry people have a readiness to confront the source of provocation, normally the partner, and many brain areas are involved in the response. Alia-Klein et al. (2020) discuss studies showing how the amygdala, anterior insula, and thalamus respond simultaneously to provocation, activating the stress response and autonomic arousal to prepare the individual for a confrontation. Thus, people who feel angry are generally drawn to retaliate. At the same time, however, there might be a need to prevent an escalation of behaviour. In order for this to happen, prefrontal cortex involvement is required, to provide conscious awareness and the ability to manage and modify aggressive tendencies. Controlling an angry outburst is very difficult to achieve and neuroimaging studies have revealed why this is the case. Research shows impairment in the mentalizing networks, and significantly, in the systems underpinning self-regulation, which are part of the anger and aggression network. With a reduction in the ability to self-regulate, expressions of hostility are more likely to occur, and further damage to the relationship is a probable outcome.

Depression in one or both partners is another common feature in unhappy couples. As we saw in the previous chapter, depressive symptoms are accompanied by the dysregulation of cortisol, OT, vasopressin, and serotonin secretion. Decreased dopamine release from the ventral tegmental area is also found with depression, and this seems to be linked to hyperactivity in the lateral habenula, a small area of the forebrain. This brain region releases two neurotransmitters discussed in detail below, GABA (gamma aminobutyric acid), and glutamate, and neuroscientific studies have indicated that these neurotransmitters have a role in depression as well (Browne et al., 2018).

Disappointment in the relationship has always emerged strongly when working with couples who stay together despite unhappiness. Feeling disappointed is particularly relevant for people who had hoped for emotional closeness and security, but then feel very let-down by their partner, whether for sexual, financial, or other reasons. Strong negative emotions pervade a relationship when people live with stress, anger, frustration, and depression. Activity in the lateral habenula has a central role in the regulation of disappointment, which is an emotional state that has received little attention in the research literature. Although there is an abundance of research into mood disorders in humans, studies into the neurobiology of disappointment are lacking. However, some indication of the neurobiology of disappointment can be gleaned from animal research. Shabel et al. (2014) studied rodents bred to show aspects of human depression, who were given a no-reward task to induce disappointment. Researchers observed changes in the lateral habenula, an area that is activated by unexpected negative experiences. They found the emotion of disappointment was signalled by the ratio of glutamate to GABA, the neurotransmitters implicated in depression, which are released simultaneously in the lateral habenula. Disappointment signalling was lower in the rodents when more GABA was released compared with glutamate and greater when more glutamate was released relative to GABA. Negative emotions are therefore increased when GABA is lower than glutamate. Kaye and Ross (2017) have described a habenula model of depression based on animal studies. This model links chronic stress to an increase in lateral habenula sensitivity, which would in turn cause a greater sensitivity to experiencing disappointment.

Researchers suggest that serotonin (an antidepressant neurotransmitter) mediates the GABA–glutamate ratio by increasing GABA release (Shabel et al., 2014), and thereby raising the likelihood of positive emotional states. Earlier research with rhesus monkeys given a no-reward task demonstrated that activity in the lateral habenula sends messages to the ventral tegmental area where it inhibits dopamine neurons (Matsumoto & Hikosaka, 2007). This aspect of lateral habenula activity could therefore have a central role in regulating the emotional impact of disappointment and adds to our understanding of how it can undermine relationships, in association with depressed mood. Extrapolating to human behaviour, in the absence of receiving the desired responses from a partner the outcome is likely to be that motivation and drive— underpinned by dopamine release—is lacking, and over time, with repeated disappointments, serious withdrawal from the partner can occur. And when levels of dopamine and serotonin are suppressed, OT release is also impaired, with a resulting negative mood state.

Summary and clinical relevance

Troubled and unhappy individuals and couples present with the whole range of sexual difficulties and form a significant group of referrals for psychosexual work. Neuroscientific evidence shows how negative emotional states contribute to reluctance for sex and withdrawal from intimate contact. Lower levels of GABA than glutamate, increased circulating cortisol, and the absence of opportunities for oxytocin and dopamine release will contribute to disappointment in the relationship.

Therapists will be aware of the importance of working on stress, anger, hostility, depression, and disappointment as a necessary first step. If these potentially damaging emotions are addressed satisfactorily, therapy can focus on couple harmony, before introducing a gradual approach to physical contact. Timing for discussing any form of mutual touch requires careful thought, because couple relationships which remain imbued with resentment can be predicted to respond badly to pleasuring and sensate focus exercises. These exercises are successful when therapy has enabled the couple to manage negative emotions and reach a "neutral", if not a positive place, for further progress to be achieved. Finding ways to think about how disappointment is expressed in the relationship in a non-blaming way may also be useful and lead to a focus on communication styles. Encouraging constructive feedback rather than constant criticism is frequently a part of the work with unhappy couples before any other methods are employed.

Case vignette

Paul and Rose

Paul and Rose were in their late fifties and had been married for thirty-five years when they requested therapy. Rose complained that Paul was remote and indifferent to her, while Paul was upset about the absence of any sexual or affectionate contact for the previous few years. Neither of them could remember when they were last intimate, although they still shared a bedroom. The couple married when young, soon after they met, and moved to London where they had two boys quite quickly. Both sons were working and lived away, although the older, Alec, had just left his girlfriend and had moved back in with his parents. Paul expressed anger and distress about the couple's lifestyle, which he said left him feeling very isolated and lonely. He worked during the week managing considerable responsibilities running a large team, but the evenings were empty. He would retreat to watch television while Rose was on the phone for hours with her friends. Rose described Paul as constantly in a bad mood and not good company. Her contact with friends was important as Paul wouldn't talk to her, and she needed to communicate. For his part, Paul said that Rose couldn't understand his work pressures and showed no interest in anything he did. He said the topics Rose chatted about were trivial and he was dismissive about her friendship group. While Rose was sad, Paul was angry and insisted he deserved more from the marriage.

In their backgrounds, Paul had an older brother with a serious psychiatric diagnosis who was in residential care for most of his adult life. His father had never come to terms with the older brother's condition and left most of the contact with the care home and psychiatric team to Paul's mother. Paul expressed anger about his father's denial of the situation which put a heavy burden on his mother, to whom Paul was very close. His father had died the previous year, and Paul was very attached to his mother, who still lived in the family home. He organised her finances and was fierce in his devotion to her needs. Rose had fallen out with her parents and older sister over arrangements for her grandmother's funeral ten years ago, and her only active family member was a cousin who she rarely saw. She described her father as a bully and her mother as weak for not standing up to him. In her view the older sister was prettier, cleverer, and favoured by her father. She had given up any hope or expectation of reuniting with her family again.

When they first met in their early twenties Rose admired Paul's confidence and ambition, while Paul was immediately drawn to Rose's vulnerability and warm personality and felt he wanted to take care of her. Paul knew from early on that Rose struggled with sexual intimacy except for the brief periods when she wanted to conceive. In terms of running the home they cooperated along traditional lines, but shared activities and intimacy had been absent for years. After the third session the couple arrived in a crisis situation because their son Alec had picked up his father Paul's phone by mistake and found compromising messages and a photo of a woman. Alec told his mother, who was extremely distressed, especially because he recognised the woman as the widow of a family friend, and the couple had been to their home. In the session Rose was distraught and wanted to focus on Paul's infidelity, while he claimed to be the neglected partner, and insisted he was entitled to some comfort after years of emotional indifference. Paul said he was always attracted to Rose and had no feelings for anyone else, but the lack of sex was creating a real problem for him. He agreed to break any further contact with the other woman, who he claimed was not important to him, and they both wanted to work on the relationship.

Couple therapy was challenging because the couple interactions remained full of blame, hurt, and heightened emotions. Rose repeatedly returned to the infidelity, while Paul continued to insist that it was only a symptom of a long-standing issue. They regularly rehearsed these themes, with both partners putting obstacles in the way of calmly discussing how to live together more amicably. Rose was reluctant to introduce any physical contact with Paul beyond a brief hug, admitting she would find sexual intimacy very difficult. She wanted to look after

Paul in other ways and had no wish to break up the family. Paul was clear that he wanted to stay with Rose and would never leave her. It seemed that both partners had brought disappointment, resentment, and anger into their couple relationships. These painful emotions were based on neural pathways that had been reinforced frequently over the years and had become embedded in the way they related. When I spoke to them about reducing negative emotions to alter neurotransmitter release and unhelpful brain connections, anger was expressed towards me for suggesting there could be a different pattern to their behaviour towards each other.

Eventually the couple agreed to spend some time talking in the evening and then to have a hug and peck on the cheek. This was problematic as Rose was resistant to being touched, causing further anger from Paul. A weekend break away was also suggested, which Rose was asked to arrange, but this did not take place either. They understood the value of engaging in positive warm interactions; however, week after week they remained stuck in the same distancing patterns. Opportunities for emotional connection with OT release were missing. Paul was troubled by the absence of affection and sex and wanted to be touched, whereas Rose was very far from resuming anything physical, so between them a compromise solution was arrived at. Although Rose would not let Paul touch her body she agreed to stroke Paul and touch his penis, without stimulating him. Rose accepted Paul's distress and she agreed he could occasionally see a sex worker, with appropriate precautions, if he had no contact with someone they knew. Such an unusual arrangement was not ideal but emerged as the least painful option in a complex situation where neither partner wanted to end the relationship, nor were they able to make any meaningful changes.

CHAPTER 9

Long-term relationships: staying together contentedly

D espite the vicissitudes of events and complexities of intimate relationships, many couples continue to receive pleasure from sharing their lives and moreover to feel in love for many years. How people manage to maintain successful loving relationships over the course of a long partnership is of considerable interest, but very little neuroscientific research has addressed this area. One significant brain imaging study by Acevedo et al. (2011) investigated the neural correlates of long-term romantic love. Their participants were heterosexual couples who fulfilled various criteria, including staying together for between ten and twenty-nine years. All the participants were sexually monogamous, and the methods used were a replication of the Aron et al. (2005) study into early-stage romantic love to allow a direct comparison, but with the addition this time of a picture of a close long-term friend. This was specifically to compare neural activity related to attachment with the partner to that with someone who was valued by the subject. As with early-stage romantic love, long-term romantic love was associated with neural activity in the dopamine rich systems—the right ventral tegmental area (VTA) and caudate—linked with motivation and reward. Bartels and Zeki (2004) had found the same pattern in their couples and, in addition, compared the imaging results with parent–infant attachment. In both conditions there was activation in overlapping brain regions of the reward system which have a high density of oxytocin and vasopressin receptors, plus deactivation of networks underpinning negative emotions and social judgement.

Romantic love (early-stage and long-term) and maternal love were therefore shown to exhibit an absence of mentalizing, indicating that the ability to assess the intentions and motives of others had become reduced. Significantly though, romantic love differed from maternal love in respect of two brain regions, the hippocampus and the hypothalamus, neither of which became active with maternal love, and are therefore considered to be unique to romantic love. Moreover, measures of sexual frequency in the Acevedo et al. (2011) study were noteworthy, showing a positive correlation with activity in the posterior hypothalamus, and in the left posterior hippocampus. Neural activity in the posterior hypothalamus is linked to sexual arousal in both genders, but the difference is that men show higher activation of the hypothalamus than women when viewing erotic films (Karama et al., 2002). Although less is known about the role of the hippocampus in relationships, the hippocampal brain region is linked to memory function, enabling consolidation from short- to long-term memory. Hippocampal activity is also reported to increase with age, which possibly results from the older brain attempting to maintain normal memory function (Blum et al., 2014). Perhaps couples who have been together lovingly for many years are able to draw on past memories and combine past and present emotions to maintain a meaningful connection, and the feeling of being in love, which can be re-evoked at times to continue throughout the relationship.

A further measure in the Acevedo et al. (2011) study, the IOS (inclusion of other in the self) scale, allowed researchers to test the self-expansion theory of motivation and cognition in close relationship development (Aron & Aron, 1986). Rapid expansion of both partners is posited to take place when they first meet due to intense conversations, typically involving self-disclosure, frequent sharing of information, and risk-taking. Such interactions can cause each person to internalise the perspectives and resources of the other as if, in a way, they become a part of themselves—thereby creating an expansion of the self—accompanied by positive feelings. If expansion decreases or disappears with time, the risk of reduced pleasure and enjoyment becomes linked to the relationship. Those couples who share new self-expanding activities will associate the excited engagement with the partner-related activity and are more likely to reinvigorate the relationship and keep their romantic love alive. Results from the above study showed a correlation between VTA activation and closeness scores on the IOS, providing evidence for the self-expansion theory.

Data from the couples who remained in love for a long period of time and reported their partnership to be highly rewarding were analysed, to demonstrate the relevance of psychobiological systems in the regulation of attachment (Acevedo et al., 2012). Researchers investigated patterns of brain activation that underpin satisfaction, empathy, positive evaluation of the other, and sustainability, and found a link between the activation of motivation and reward evaluation regions (VTA, caudate, prefrontal cortex, and orbitofrontal cortex) and measures of satisfaction. Relationship stability was correlated with activation in the caudate, medial orbitofrontal cortex, and cingulate regions, and there was an interesting link between behaviour directed at a goal and the positive evaluation of the self and others. Responding to a partner's needs was indicated by neural activity in areas implicated in empathy and responsiveness. Both of these are important aspects of an attachment system that maintains stable relationships. Reward, satisfaction, and stability were underpinned by brain systems that promote two relevant aspects of individual functioning: decreased impulsivity and general well-being. These would both be predicted to enhance a close relationship. A further link between relationship quality and physical and mental health was shown by reduced activation of a brain region associated with severe depression (subcallosal cingulate gyrus). Overall, the study provided neurobiological evidence confirming that different brain regions underpin romantic love (VTA) and attachment (globus pallidus and substantia nigra), while showing their coexistence for those fortunate couples who remain together in stable bonds over the long term.

In a later study designed to investigate the biological mechanisms involved in the relationship features that impact on romantic love, Acevedo et al. (2020) reported a correlation between sexual frequency, scores on a romantic love scale, and satisfaction with the relationship, albeit in couples who had just married and one year later. Using the same methods as Aron et al. (2005), who studied early-stage romantic love, Acevedo et al. (2020) compared participants' brain responses when viewing a photo of the partner in an fMRI scanner with a photo of a familiar acquaintance. Similar again to the findings of Bartels and Zeki (2004), brain networks associated with judgement of others and negative emotions were deactivated. Moreover, results showed that sexual activity between couples not only promoted physical health but also contributed to experiences such as emotional intimacy, meaning-making, awareness, and trust. These are higher order cognitive processes that are linked with pleasurable sex through the activation of specific brain areas (the inferior frontal gyrus, temporal, and parietal areas) associated with complex psychological phenomenon (Acevedo et al., 2019). Research using only questionnaires has also explored the key factors enabling couples to remain together harmoniously, by examining the role of sexual contact and affection in couple satisfaction, with a focus on well-being both within and between partners. A series of studies indicated that interpersonal warmth, mutual respect, and affection, achieved through sexual activity, were central to a sense of well-being, and to relationship satisfaction in the long term (Debrot et al., 2017).

We can see that neural processes are relevant for satisfaction over the years, but an additional question is whether there are any genetic factors that could contribute to sustaining love over the course of a relationship. Indeed, Acevedo et al. (2020) did find evidence of a link between certain genetic variants, and activation of the brain's reward system, with romantic love. Researchers analysed specific polymorphisms (variations in a gene sequence) of oxytocin, vasopressin, and dopamine genes by taking saliva samples from the participants, and they also assessed the relationship quality via self-report measures. Identified polymorphisms of oxytocin, vasopressin, and dopamine genes were found to be associated with VTA activation in response to the partner only. Although this research looked at couples when they had just married and one year later, the selected polymorphisms were considered to constitute evidence of a genetic influence on relationship maintenance. From these various studies we can see there is a growing body of research showing that a combination of genetic factors, higher-order cognitive processes, and the brain's reward system are all involved in the ability to maintain romantic love relationships.

Summary and clinical relevance

Neuroscientific research adds another dimension to our understanding of the features enabling couples to create and maintain successful relationships. In particular, activation in the ventral tegmental area and caudate for dopamine release, and the hypothalamus for sexual arousal, were significant features of contended couples. Ongoing physical and sexual contact, whether or not intercourse is included, provides pleasure and meaningful experiences. Finding ways to share activities and, if possible, to develop new interests, will have a role in continuing the self-expansion that is so important for the couple bond. Recalling memories of rewarding times together in the past might also play a part in consolidating emotional connections in the present. There is evidence too that reflective and self–other processes, along with the release of oxytocin and opioids previously described, are part of the neural systems humans have evolved to sustain love in a long-term partnership. As might be expected, impulse control and responsivity to the needs of a partner are implicated in staying together harmoniously. Couples who are able to continue activation of the neural regions linked with long-term intimate relationships confirm how humans can achieve a sense of meaning in life through closeness, trust, and affection with a partner, reinforcing the focus on these goals in psychosexual therapy.

Case vignette

Daisy and Brad

Daisy, fifty-five, and Brad, fifty-eight, were married for thirty years when they started psychosexual therapy to address Daisy's loss of interest in sex. In general they were a harmonious couple who enjoyed music and gardening together, and they had a daughter, Dawn, who was nineteen. Throughout their relationship sexual contact was infrequent. Brad would initiate every few months and Daisy was able to respond because she liked the closeness, although she had never wanted to stimulate Brad and did not climax. For the previous two years, however, Daisy's willingness had declined, and she was finding it increasingly difficult to feel comfortable with anything beyond a hug. When they did progress to intercourse the experience left her with a flat and hollow feeling.

For a while she tried to hide it, until Brad noticed her crying after the last occasion, which left him confused and hurt. He was adamant that he would never persuade Daisy to have sex if she felt uncomfortable. She had had no sexual partners before marriage, and Brad had had one sexual experience with someone he dated for a short while. He was drawn to Daisy's gentle and caring nature and said sex was not the most important part of their relationship, although he hated feeling unwanted. As a couple they were unsure about whether to continue trying to have a sexual relationship as it was causing distress for both of them.

In Daisy's background she had a brother, six years older, who she disliked intensely and avoided, so they rarely saw each other. Her mother was a meek and quiet person, but her father was short-tempered and not very involved with family life. Brad was brought up by a single mother, his father having left when Brad was eight, and contact with him was only once or twice a year as he grew up. Talking about her brother caused distress for Daisy, because he and his friends used to tease her, especially as she started to develop physically. During therapy there was a death in Daisy's family, and she became very stressed at the thought of the funeral where she would see her brother. Afterwards she brought a dream in which her brother and his friends pushed her onto a bed, touched her, showed her their erections, and one boy made her touch him. Daisy was full of shame and embarrassment when recounting the dream because it scared her, and she didn't know if the event actually happened. As we explored the dream and discussed more about her childhood, Daisy recalled other episodes of feeling scared when her brother and his friends were in the house. From the strength of her reactions to her brother it did seem probable that she had been subjected to a sexually traumatising experience of that kind as a child, which had then been repressed. Whether the scenario had taken place or was a fear that had reached conscious awareness through the dream, this frightening sexual scene was clearly meaningful to her. Of significance too, Daisy's issues with sex had begun when Dawn, their daughter, had her first boyfriend and was introduced to his friends. I suggested that Daisy's identification with Dawn had connected with fears about male demands for sex and provoked an involuntary withdrawal response, as a form of self-protection. Brad was not a man who exerted pressure for sex, and he was dismayed about where this left him.

We discussed the connection between the orbitofrontal cortex, which assesses events, and the amygdala, the core fear system in the brain, which unconsciously appraises situations based on past experiences, leading to rapid emotional and physiological responses. This prepares us to fight, flee, or freeze, and in Daisy's case the freeze response could account for her inability to respond and her reluctance for sexual contact. Brad was able to see that Daisy's distress was not a rejection of him, rather it was an involuntary reaction to an earlier event that was stored in her amygdala and was re-evoked by current events. Once the memory was recalled, through the dream, it had reached the hippocampus, allowing conscious awareness, so that Daisy was able to process and manage her fears. On the subcortical level, the hippocampus has input to the hypothalamus, enabling regulation of cortisol production. Our co-construction in the sessions of a narrative that made sense of Daisy's sexual anxieties enabled the couple to progress. I suggested they could try to increase eye contact in bed to enable Daisy to confirm Brad as a safe partner. With a gradual approach to physical contact, Daisy learned to feel calm with Brad again, to hug in bed and to gradually allow him to stroke her. Sensate focus exercises were an option, although the couple agreed together that penetrative sex was not important to them. They could both enjoy some mutual caressing and Brad no longer felt unwanted. Once Dawn left home they decided to start ballroom dancing classes, which was something they had previously considered but not had time to do and was an activity that could continue their pleasure in shared activities.

CHAPTER 10

Concluding comments

Managing intimate sexual behaviours causes concern to most of us over the life course, and finding out more about the brain processes involved in relationship dynamics might help to address issues and to negotiate the inevitable changes. Many complex factors interweave to create the powerful human drive to love, connect, relate, and mate with one another. Neuroscience has begun to explore these basic urges, and my aim with this book was to describe the current research as it pertains to love, intimacy, and sex. However, a large amount of literature has now accumulated on the neural correlates that preserve homeostasis for optimal functioning. There are multiple intricate cross connections, many of which currently remain a mystery: an exhaustive review would be too big a task. Nevertheless, the main topics of relevance to psychosexual therapy have been included here. I have intentionally avoided an attempt to link neural network activity with specific treatment approaches for all the different sexual problems, preferring to leave each clinician to decide whether the ideas could be used in ways that enrich their own style with clients. How this is done will depend on the nature of the work and personalities of both the therapists and the clients.

Although psychosexual therapists may not be at the stage where knowledge of neurobiology is essential for effective work, my hope is that the research presented in each chapter shows how neural correlates linking emotions, thoughts, and behaviours are central to sexual expression. And the more clinicians are aware of how these pathways underpin sexuality, the better equipped we are to facilitate positive change. Cozolino (2017) describes psychotherapy as impacting dysregulated neural circuits through the creation of individually tailored enriched environments, to build and regulate the brain, and to stimulate and guide neuroplastic processes. In his view the success of psychotherapy depends on the extent to which it brings about change in relevant neural circuits and alters brain chemistry.

In the area of couple therapy, Fishbane (2013) is convinced that neuroscience is crucial for understanding how our brain–body connections affect relationships, particularly if couples are unable to manage their reactivity to each other when angry or distressed. Fishbane's (2013) neuroeducation approach includes describing how prefrontal cortex activity can calm the amygdala as a method of helping clints to understand their own inner processes, and to position self-regulation at the core. Replacing automatic emotionally driven behaviour with conscious reflection is an ongoing struggle in an intimate relationship, where we are at our most vulnerable. An awareness of the distinction between automaticity and thoughtful choice, and a description of the brain areas underpinning these responses, can offer insights from neurobiology that reinforce the ability to alter unhelpful behaviours.

One of the defining aspects of human existence is the attempt to achieve homeostasis, the state of a positively regulated life. Homeostasis is maintained by the brain's body-sensing regions continuously receiving signals with which to map our ongoing biological state (Damasio, 2000). Emotions and drives are also part of our homeostatic regulation. On the level of neurobiology, we have seen how neurochemicals and neuronal activation enable us to balance arousal and inhibition: dopamine and cortisol balance excitement and stress, GABA and glutamate balance reward and disappointment, and amygdala and prefrontal activity balance dysregulated feelings with reasoned thinking. When considering intimate relationships, our attempts to manage opposing emotions such as love or hate, approach or withdrawal, desire or distaste, can be a challenge. From the perspective of sexual behaviour, the brain–genital connections which serve to stimulate blood flow to pelvic organs are central to sexual expression, and emotional and physical homeostasis will greatly aid this process. Dopamine has a key role in producing motivation, sexual arousal, and pleasure in all aspects of relationship functioning, but is readily decreased with negative emotions. Descriptions of this neurotransmitter can add weight to attempts to increase novelty, shared activities, and stimulating pursuits to couple activity. Similarly, by considering how oxytocin can promote trust, confidence, and empathy through sensitive exchanges and touch, we can add a neuroscience basis to sensate focus exercises. For some couples I have found that discussing the three distinct but connected systems that underpin mating drives (lust, attraction, and attachment) can clarify some conflictual emotions, and possibly increase tolerance of their own and their partner's sexual drives and feelings for others to whom they might become drawn. Taking into account basic concepts in neurobiology can serve to reduce some of the guilt a partner can experience when, for example, they lose interest in sex due to serious disharmony or during a difficult phase in a relationship. At such times, withdrawal due to a sense of insecurity or anxiety is an automatic protective measure, driven by the memory stores of the amygdala, rather than a conscious act designed to cause pain. Uncovering the sources of a loss of interest in sex is part of the cognitive preparation for modifications, and encourages hippocampal–cortical network activity, to reduce the stress related to intimacy.

Psychosexual and couple work, as with all therapy, aims to create emotional and behavioural changes. These changes occur through neuroplasticity and neurogenesis, the rewiring of neurons and the growth of new neurons, in response to our physical and social world, including the therapy context. We can feel encouraged to know that while the early infant years are particularly sensitive periods for neuronal growth, the brain has the capacity to retain plasticity throughout the life course and can continue to mature and develop. Intimate relationships require the ongoing creation of new neural pathways, a process that has been called the interpersonal sculpting of the brain (Cozolino, 2017). People need time in each other's company for this to happen. As we saw in Chapter 6, regular communication and physical contact facilitate the biobehavioural synchrony that characterises harmonious relationships, including intimacy and pleasurable sex. Siegel (2010) stresses the role of practice and repetition for lasting change to be achieved. Repetition stimulates the growth of myelin sheaths round neurons to greatly increase the efficiency and speed of signals transmitted in the nervous system. Conversely if neural pathways remain unused they gradually fade and decay with time, as a process of synaptic pruning occurs. Discussing this with clients can give some optimism for people who want to achieve real progress. Understanding how mental training creates efficient neural networks can provide confidence for the therapist too.

There is much more to learn as further research is undertaken, and neuroscience will hopefully provide increasing insights into intimate relationships. With new knowledge, hypotheses linking brain mechanisms with sexuality can be updated in light of the material, and potentially incorporated into neuropsychosexual therapy alongside currently used methods. My view is that neuroscience has much to offer clinicians in all fields. A method to integrate neuropsychoanalysis with classic psychoanalytic treatment has been proposed (Mosri, 2021), and the time seems right for psychosexual therapy to integrate neuroscientific knowledge with well-established approaches for psychosexual problems.

I hope that others will find, as I have, that a neuropsychosexual approach can influence clinical work both subtly and directly, add depth of a different kind to the therapeutic dialogue, and provide valuable insights to clients struggling with intimacy.

Glossary

Allele: two or more alternative forms of a gene at a specific location in the genetic sequence.

Amygdala: alert, alarm, and integrative centre, receives inputs from all senses, plays a central role in immediate responses to stimuli, anxiety-related memory, and generating strong violent emotion. Signals from the amygdala to the hypothalamus stimulate the fight, flight, or freeze response.

Anterior cingulate cortex (ACC): a region with high concentrations of sex-hormone receptors. Involved with complex cognitive functions, emotion, empathy, decision-making, impulse control, consciousness.

Anterior insula (AI): associated with empathy and awareness, risky decisions, interoception (awareness of physiological state of the body).

Beta-endorphins: endogenous opioids released in different brain regions, that bind to mu-opioid receptors located throughout the nervous system, including the amygdala and hypothalamus. Beta-endorphins reduce stress, regulate emotion, pain, and motivation, and maintain homeostasis.

Caudate nucleus: executive functioning, decision-making processes, procedural learning, associative learning, and inhibitory control of action, part of the reward system, highly innervated by dopaminergic neurons.

Cingulate gyrus: part of the cingulate cortex involved in emotion processing, memory, linking behaviours to positive outcomes, executive function.

Cortex: outer layer of the brain containing specialised areas in humans for higher-level language, decision-making, and reasoning functions.

Cortisol: stress producing hormone released from the adrenal glands when stimulated by the hypothalamus; increases availability of glucose for the fight, freeze, or fleeing response.

Dopamine (DA): neurotransmitter produced by the ventral tegmental area and hypothalamus, important for executive function, determines feelings of pleasure, reward and motivation, arousal, excitement, drive, sends messages between nerve cells, facilitates striving, focus, and finding things interesting.

Globus pallidus (GP): controls constant regulation of movement.

Hippocampus: vital for conscious functioning, short- to long-term memory consolidation, regulates learning, motivation, spatial memory, encodes emotional context from the amygdala.

HPA axis (hypothalamic–pituitary–adrenal): major neuroendocrine system consisting of the hypothalamus, pituitary gland, and the adrenals (small, conical organs on top of the kidneys). HPA axis interactions control responses to stress and regulate many body processes, including digestion, the immune system, mood and emotions, sexuality.

Hypothalamus: hormone releasing area of the emotional brain, controls internal balance (homeostasis)—also controls many other vital functions, parenting and attachment behaviours, emotions, thirst, fatigue, body temperature, hunger, sleep cycles, and circadian rhythms.

Lateral habenula: forebrain region, responds when expectations are not met.

Mesolimbic pathway: dopaminergic pathway in the brain connecting the ventral tegmental area in the midbrain to the ventral striatum of the basal ganglia in the forebrain; promotes primary pleasurable rewards essential for survival and homeostasis, such as eating and mating.

Mu-opioid receptor (MOR) one of the opioid receptors that releases endogenous opioids as beta-endorphins.

Noradrenaline (NA): neurotransmitter—mobilises the brain and body for action, increases heart rate, arousal, and alertness.

Nucleus accumbens (NAcc): processes rewarding and reinforcing stimuli, involved in cognitive processing of motivation and aversion.

Orbitofrontal cortex (OFC): part of the prefrontal cortex, a key site involved in goal directed behaviour, affect, making decisions, selective memory retrieval, the evaluation of rewards.

Oxytocin (OT): neuropeptide/neurotransmitter for emotional connection, trust, confidence, bonding, orgasm, pleasure, stress reduction; manufacture is stimulated by oestrogen.

Pelvic organ stimulating centre (POSC): a group of neurons in the brainstem driven by the PAG—generates micturition, defecation, and sexual activities.

Periaqueductal grey (PAG): integrates behavioural responses to internal (e.g. pain) or external (e.g. threat) stressors—receives information from all pelvic organs, the primary control centre for descending pain modulation.

Polymorphism: variation in the genetic sequence.

Prefrontal cortex (PFC): involved in decision-making, executive function, planning, complex cognitive behaviour, prediction of outcomes.

Serotonin: a neurotransmitter, carries messages throughout the brain and body, modulates cognition, memory, mood, sleep, sexual desire, vasoconstriction, and various physiological processes.

Subcortex: area for processing more primitive functions and emotions, continually interacting with cortical areas, aids suppression of anger.

Substantia nigra (SN): central role in brain function, including learning, reward-seeking, motor-planning, eye movement, and addiction.

Temporal lobe: vital for understanding language, visual memory, all sensory input including pain and auditory stimuli, remembering emotions and conscious memories, controlling unconscious and apparently automatic reactions, such as appetite, thirst, hunger.

Thalamus: regulates alertness and consciousness, relays sensory and motor signals

Vasopressin (VP): neuropeptide/neurotransmitter for trust, empathy, social memories, defensive behaviour, mobilisation, aggression, sexual bonding; manufacture is stimulated by testosterone.

Ventral tegmental area (VTA): reward and motivation, immediate responses to fear, and anxiety-related memory, receives inputs from all senses.

References

Abernathy, K., Chandler, L. J., & Woodward, J. J. (2010). Alcohol and the prefrontal cortex. *International Review of Neurobiology, 9*: 289–320.

Acevedo, B. P., Aron, A., Fisher, H. E., & Brown, L. L. (2011). Neural correlates of long-term intense romantic love. *Social Cognitive and Affective Neuroscience, 7*(2): 145–159.

Acevedo, B. P., Aron, A., Fisher, H. E., & Brown, L. L. (2012). Neural correlates of marital satisfaction and well-being: Reward, empathy, and affect. *Clinical Neuropsychiatry: Journal of Treatment Evaluation, 9*(1): 20–31.

Acevedo, B. P., Poulin, M. J., Collins, N. L., & Brown, L. L. (2020). After the honeymoon: Neural and genetic correlates of romantic love in newlywed marriages. *Frontiers in Psychology, 11.* doi:10.3389/fpsyg.2020.00634.

Acevedo, B. P., Poulin, M. J., Geher, G., Grafton, S., & Brown, L. L. (2019). The neural and genetic correlates of satisfying sexual activity in heterosexual pair-bonds. *Brain and Behavior, 9*(6): e01289.

Alia-Klein, N., Gan, G., Gilam, G., Bezek, J., Bruno, A., Denson, T., Hendler, T., Lowe, L., Mariotti, V., Muscatello, M., Palumbo, S., Pellegrini, S., Pietrini, P., Rizzo, A., & Verona, E. (2020). The feeling of anger: From brain networks to linguistic expressions. *Neuroscience & Biobehavioral Reviews, 108*: 480–497.

Aron, A., & Aron, E. N. (1986). *Love and the Expansion of Self: Understanding Attraction and Satisfaction.* New York: Hemisphere/Harper & Row.

Aron, A., Fisher, H., Mashek, D. J., Strong, G., Li, H., & Brown, L. L. (2005). Reward, motivation, and emotion systems associated with early-stage intense romantic love. *Journal of Neurophysiology*, *94*(1): 327–337.

Banihashemi, L., Wallace, M. L., Peng, C. W., Stinley, M. M., Germain, A., & Herringa, R. J. (2020). Interactions between childhood maltreatment and combat exposure trauma on stress-related activity within the cingulate cortex: A pilot study. *Military Psychology*, *32*(2): 176–185.

Bartels, A., & Zeki, S. (2000). The neural basis of romantic love. *NeuroReport*, *11*(17): 3829–3834.

Bartels, A., & Zeki, S. (2004). The neural correlates of maternal and romantic love. *NeuroImage*, *21*(3): 1155–1166.

Baskerville, T. A., & Douglas, A. J. (2010). Dopamine and oxytocin interactions underlying behaviors: Potential contributions to behavioral disorders. *CNS Neuroscience & Therapeutics*, *16*(3): e92–e123.

Basson, R. (2001). Using a different model for female sexual response to address women's problematic low sexual desire. *Journal of Sex & Marital Therapy*, *27*(5): 395–403.

Basson, R., Leiblum, S., Brotto, L., Derogatis L., Fourcroy, J., Fugl-Meyer, K., Graziottin, A., Heiman, J. R., Laan, E., Meston, C., Schover, L., van Lankveld, J., & Weijmar Schultz, W. (2004). Revised definitions of women's sexual dysfunction. *Journal of Sexual Medicine*, *1*(1): 40–48.

Bayerl, D. S., & Bosch, O. J. (2018). Brain vasopressin signaling modulates aspects of maternal behavior in lactating rats. *Genes, Brain and Behavior*, *18*(1): e12517.

Berretz, G., Cebula, C., Wortelmann, B. M., Papadopoulou, P., Wolf, O. T., Ocklenburg, S., & Packheiser, J. (2022). Romantic partner embraces reduce cortisol release after acute stress induction in women but not in men. *PLoS One*, *17*(5): e0266887.

Binik, Y. M., & Hall, K. S. K. (Eds.) (2014). *Principles and Practice of Sex Therapy* (5th edn.). New York: Guilford.

Bittoni, C., & Kiesner, J. (2022). Sexual desire in women: Paradoxical and nonlinear associations with anxiety and depressed mood. *Archives of Sexual Behavior*, *51*(8): 3807–3822.

Blair, R. J. R. (2012). Considering anger from a cognitive neuroscience perspective. *Wiley Interdisciplinary Reviews: Cognitive Science*, *3*(1): 65–74.

Blum, S., Habeck, C., Steffener, J., Razlighi, Q., & Stern, Y. (2014). Functional connectivity of the posterior hippocampus is more dominant as we age. *Cognitive Neuroscience*, *5*(3–4): 150–159.

de Boer, A., van Buel, E. M., & Ter Horst, G. J. (2012). Love is more than just a kiss: A neurobiological perspective on love and affection. *Neuroscience, 201*: 114–124.

Brizendine, L. (2006). *The Female Brain*. London: Bantam.

Brizendine, L. (2010). *The Male Brain*. London: Bantam.

Brotto, L. A., & Yule, M. A. (2011). Physiological and subjective sexual arousal in self-identified asexual women. *Archives of Sexual Behavior, 40*: 699–712.

Browne, C. A., Hammack, R., & Lucki, I. (2018). Dysregulation of the lateral habenula in major depressive disorder. *Frontiers in Synaptic Neuroscience, 10*(46): doi: 10.3389/fnsyn.2018.00046.

Carmichael, M. S., Humbert, T. R., Dixon, J., Palmisano, G., Greenleaf, W., & Davidson, J. M. (1987). Plasma oxytocin increases in the human sexual response. *Journal of Clinical Endocrinology and Metabolism, 64*: 27–31.

Carter, C. S. (1992). Oxytocin and sexual behavior. *Neuroscience & Biobehavioral Reviews, 16*(2): 131–144.

Carter, C. S. (2017a). The oxytocin–vasopressin pathway in the context of love and fear. *Frontiers in Endocrinology, 8*: 356.

Carter, C. S. (2017b). The role of oxytocin and vasopressin in attachment. *Psychodynamic Psychiatry, 45*(4): 499–517.

Cera, N., Delli Pizzi, S., Di Pierro, E. D., Gambi, F., Tartaro, A., Vicentini, C., Galatioto, G. P., Romani, G. L., & Ferretti, A. (2012). Macrostructural alterations of subcortical grey matter in psychogenic erectile dysfunction. *PLoS One, 7*(6): e39118.

Cherkas, L. F., Oelsner, E. C., Mak, Y. T., Valdes, A., & Spector, T. D. (2005). Genetic influences on female infidelity and number of sexual partners in humans: A linkage and association study of the role of the vasopressin receptor gene (AVPR1A). *Twin Research: The Official Journal of the International Society for Twin Studies, 7*(6): 649–658.

Coan, J. A., Schaefer, H. S., & Davidson, R. J. (2006). Lending a hand. *Psychological Science, 17*(12): 1032–1039.

Cozolino, L. (2017). *The Neuroscience of Psychotherapy: Healing the Social Brain*. New York: W. W. Norton.

Damasio, A. R. (2000). *The Feeling of What Happens: Body, Emotion and the Making of Consciousness*. New York: Random House.

Damasio, A. R. (2010). *Self Comes to Mind. Constructing the Conscious Brain*. New York: Pantheon.

Debrot, A., Meuwly, N., Muise, A., Impett, E. A., & Schoebi, D. (2017). More than just sex: Affection mediates the association between sexual activity and well-being. *Personality and Social Psychology Bulletin, 43*(3): 287–299.

Defreyne, J., Elaut, E., Kreukels, B., Fisher, A. D., Castellini, G., Staphorsius, A., Den Heijer, M., Heylens, G., T'Sjoen, G. (2020). Sexual desire changes in transgender individuals upon initiation of hormone treatment: Results from the longitudinal European Network for the Investigation of Gender Incongruence. *Journal of Sexual Medicine, 17*(4): 812–825.

Ditzen, B., Schaer, M., Gabriel, B., Bodenmann, G., Ehlert, U., & Heinrichs, M. (2009). Intranasal oxytocin increases positive communication and reduces cortisol levels during couple conflict. *Biological Psychiatry, 65*(9): 728–731.

Dobs, A. S., Matsumoto, A. M., Wang, C., & Kipnes, M. S. (2004). Short-term pharmacokinetic comparison of a novel testosterone buccal system and a testosterone gel in testosterone deficient men. *Current Medical Research and Opinion, 20*(5): 729–738.

Doss, B. D., & Rhoades, G. K. (2017). The transition to parenthood: impact on couples' romantic relationships. *Current Opinion in Psychology, 13*: 25–28.

Eisenberger, N. I. (2015). Social pain and the brain: Controversies, questions, and where to go from here. *Annual Review of Psychology, 66*(1): 601–629.

Elliott, R. (2000). Dissociable functions in the medial and lateral orbitofrontal cortex: Evidence from human neuroimaging studies. *Cerebral Cortex, 10*(3): 308–317.

Feldman, R. (2017). The neurobiology of human attachments. *Trends in Cognitive Sciences, 21*(2): 80–99.

Ferris, L. J., Jetten, J., Hornsey, M., & Bastian, B. (2019). Feeling hurt: Revisiting the relationship between social and physical pain. *Review of General Psychology, 23*(3): 320–335.

Fishbane, M. D. (2013). *Loving with the Brain in Mind: Neurobiology and Couple Therapy*. New York: W. W. Norton.

Fisher, H. E. (1998). Lust, attraction, and attachment in mammalian reproduction. *Human Nature, 9*(1): 23–52.

Fisher, H. E. (1999). *The First Sex: The Natural Talents of Women and How They are Changing the World*. New York: Random House.

Fisher, H. E. (2004). *Why We Love: The Nature and Chemistry of Romantic Love*. New York: Henry Holt.

Fisher, H. E. (2011). *Why Him? Why Her?* Oxford: Oneworld.

Fisher, H. E., Aron, A., & Brown, L. L. (2005). Romantic love: An fMRI study of a neural mechanism for mate choice. *Journal of Comparative Neurology, 493*(1): 58–62.

Fisher, H. E., Aron, A., & Brown, L. L. (2006). Romantic love: A mammalian brain system for mate choice. *Philosophical Transactions of the Royal Society B: Biological Sciences, 361*(1476): 2173–2186.

Fisher, H. E., Brown, L. L., Aron, A., Strong, G., & Mashek, D. (2010). Reward, addiction, and emotion regulation systems associated with rejection in love. *Journal of Neurophysiology, 104*(1): 51–60.

Fleming, A. S., Corter, C., Stallings, J., & Steiner, M. (2002). Testosterone and prolactin are associated with emotional responses to infant cries in new fathers. *Hormones and Behavior, 42*(4): 399–413.

Fraley, R. C., Waller, N. G., & Brennan, K. A. (2000). An item-response theory analysis of self-report measures of adult attachment. *Journal of Personality and Social Psychology, 78*: 350–365.

Fries, A. B. W., Ziegler, T. E., Kurian, J. R., Jacoris, S., & Pollak, S. D. (2005). Early experience in humans is associated with changes in neuropeptides critical for regulating social behavior. *Proceedings of the National Academy of Sciences, 102*(47): 17237–17240.

Garcia, J. R., MacKillop, J., Aller, E. L., Merriwether, A. M., Wilson, D. S., & Lum, J. K. (2010). Associations between dopamine D4 receptor gene variation with both infidelity and sexual promiscuity. *PLoS One, 5*(11): e14162.

Gerhardt, S. (2004). *Why Love Matters*. London: Routledge.

Gillen, M. M., & Markey, C. H. (2019). A review of research linking body image and sexual well-being. *Body Image, 31*: 294–301.

Giotakos, O. (2020). Neurobiology of emotional trauma. *Psychiatriki, 31*(2): 162–171.

Gregory, R., Cheng, H., Rupp, H. A., Sengelaub, D. R., & Heiman, J. R. (2015). Oxytocin increases VTA activation to infant and sexual stimuli in nulliparous and postpartum women. *Hormones and Behavior, 69*: 82–88.

Hamilton, L. D., & Meston, C. M. (2013). Chronic stress and sexual function in women. *Journal of Sexual Medicine, 10*(10): 2443–2454.

Hamilton, L. D, Rellini, A. H., & Meston, C. M. (2008). Cortisol, sexual arousal, and affect in response to sexual stimuli. *Journal of Sexual Medicine, 5*(9): 2111–2118.

Handy, A. B., Reinhart, B. K., & Meston, C. M. (2020). The relationship between subjective and physiological sexual arousal in women with and without arousal concerns. *Journal of Sex & Marital Therapy, 46*(5): 447–459.

Hatfield, E., & Sprecher, S. (1986). Measuring passionate love in intimate relationships. *Journal of Adolescence, 9*(4): 383–410.

Heiman, J. R., & Maravilla, K. R. (2007). Female sexual arousal response using serial magnetic resonance imaging with initial comparisons to vaginal photoplethysmography: Overview and evaluation. In: E. Janssen (Ed.), *The Psychophysiology of Sex* (pp. 103–128). Bloomington, IN: Indiana University Press.

Hewitt, J. K. (2012). Editorial policy on candidate gene association and candidate gene-by-environment interaction studies of complex traits. *Behavior Genetics, 42*: 1–2.

Hiller, J. (1993). Psychoanalytic concepts and psychosexual therapy: A suggested integration. *Sexual and Marital Therapy, 8*: 9–26.

Hiller, J. (1996). Female sexual arousal and its impairment: The psychodynamics of non-organic coital pain. *Sexual and Marital Therapy, 11*(1): 55–76.

Hiller, J. (2004). Speculations on the links between feelings, emotions, and sexual behaviour: Are vasopressin and oxytocin involved? *Sexual and Relationship Therapy, 19*(4): 393–412.

Hiller, J. (2005). Gender differences in sexual motivation. *Journal of Men's Health & Gender, 2*(3): 339–345.

Hiller, J. (2006). Loss of sexual interest and negative states of mind. In: J. Hiller, H. Wood, & W. Bolton (Eds), *Sex, Mind, and Emotion: Innovation in Psychological Theory & Practice*. London: Karnac.

Hipp, L. E., Kane Low, L., & van Anders, S. M. (2012). Exploring women's postpartum sexuality: Social, psychological, relational, and birth-related contextual factors. *Journal of Sexual Medicine, 9*(9): 2330–2341.

Holstege, G. (2016). How the emotional motor system controls the pelvic organs. *Sexual Medicine Reviews, 4*(4): 303–328.

Holstege, G., & Huynh, H. K. (2011). Brain circuits for mating behavior in cats and brain activations and de-activations during sexual stimulation and ejaculation and orgasm in humans. *Hormones and Behavior, 59*(5): 702–707.

Holstege, G., Georgiadis, J. R., Paans, A. M. J., Memers, L. C., van der Graat, F. H. C. E., & Reinders, A. A. T. S. (2003). Brain activation during human male ejaculation. *Journal of Neuroscience, 23*(27): 9185–9193.

Hsu, D. T., Sanford, B. J., Meyers, K. K., Love, T. M., Hazlett, K. E., Wang, H., Ni, L., Walker, S. J., Mickey, B. J., Korycinski, S. T., Koeppe, R. A., Crocker, J. K., Langenecker, S. A., & Zubieta, J. K. (2013). Response of the μ-opioid system to social rejection and acceptance. *Molecular Psychiatry, 18*(11): 1211–1217.

Hsu, D. T., Sankar, A., Malik, M. A., Langenecker, S. A., Mickey, B. J., & Love, T. M. (2020). Common neural responses to romantic rejection and acceptance in healthy adults. *Social Neuroscience, 15*(5): 571–583.

Hughes, S. M., Harrison, M. A., & Gallup Jr., G. G. (2007). Sex differences in romantic kissing among college students: An evolutionary perspective. *Evolutionary Psychology, 5*(3): 612–631.

Ishunina, T. A., & Swaab, D. F. (1999). Vasopressin and oxytocin neurons of the human supraoptic and paraventricular nucleus: Size changes in relation to age and sex. *Journal of Clinical Endocrinology and Metabolism, 84*(12): 4637–4644.

Kagerer, S., Klucken, T., Wehrum, S., Zimmermann, M., Schienle, A., Walter, B., Vaitl. C., & Stark, R. (2011). Neural activation toward erotic stimuli in homosexual and heterosexual males. *Journal of Sexual Medicine, 8*(11): 3132–3143.

Kaltenboeck, A., & Harmer, C. (2018). The neuroscience of depressive disorders: A brief review of the past and some considerations about the future. *Brain and Neuroscience Advances, 2*: 239821281879926.

Karama, S., Lecours, A. R., Leroux, J.-M., Bourgouin, P., Beaudoin, G., Joubert, S., & Beauregard, M. (2002). Areas of brain activation in males and females during viewing of erotic film excerpts. *Human Brain Mapping, 16*(1): 1–13.

Kaye, A., & Ross, D. A. (2017). The habenula: Darkness, disappointment, and depression. *Biological Psychiatry, 81*(4): e27–e28.

Keltner, D. (2009). *Born to Be Good*. New York: W. W. Norton.

King, A. P., Muzik, M., Hamilton, L., Taylor, A. B., Rosenblum, K. L., & Liberzon, I. (2016). Dopamine receptor gene DRD4 7-Repeat allele X maternal sensitivity interaction on child externalizing behavior problems: Independent replication of effects at 18 months. *PLoS One, 11*(8): e0160473.

Komisaruk, B. R., Beyer, C., & Whipple, B. (2008). Orgasm. *The Psychologist, 21*(2): 100–103.

Kross, E., Berman, M. C., Mischel, W., Smith, E. E., & Wager, T. D. (2011). Social rejection shares somatosensory representations with physical pain. *Proceedings of the National Academy of Sciences, 108*(15): 6270–6275.

Laan, E., & Everaerd, W. T. A. M. (1995). Determinants of female sexual arousal: Psychophysiological theory and data. *Annual Review of Sex Research, 6*(1): 32–76.

Laan, E., van Driel, E. M., & van Lunsen, R. H. W. (2008). Genital responsiveness in healthy women with and without sexual arousal disorder. *Journal of Sexual Medicine, 5*(6): 1424–1435.

Leiblum, S. R. (2007). Sex therapy today: Current issues and future perspectives. In: S. R. Leiblum (Ed.), *Principles and Practice of Sex Therapy* (pp. 3–22). New York: Guilford.

Leknes, S., & Tracey, I. (2008). A common neurobiology for pain and pleasure. *Nature Reviews Neuroscience, 9*(4): 314–320.

Lim, M. M., & Young, L. J. (2004). Vasopressin-dependent neural circuits underlying pair bond formation in the monogamous prairie vole. *Neuroscience, 125*(1): 35–45.

Marazziti, D. (1999). Biological basis of OCD and OCD-related disorders. *European Neuropsychopharmacology, 9*: 185.

Marazziti, D., & Baroni, S. (2012). Romantic love: The mystery of its biological roots. *Clinical Neuropsychiatry, 9*(1): 14–19.

Marazziti, D., & Canale, D. (2004). Hormonal changes when falling in love. *Psychoneuroendocrinology, 29*(7): 931–936.

Marazziti, D., Dell'Osso, B., Baroni, S., Mungai, F., Catena, M., Rucci, P., Albanese, F., Giannaccini, G., Betti, L., Fabbrini, L., Italiani, P., Del Debbio, A., Lucacchini, A., & Dell'Osso, L. (2006). A relationship between oxytocin and anxiety of romantic attachment. *Clinical Practice and Epidemiology in Mental Health, 2*(1): article 28.

Matsumoto, M., & Hikosaka, O. (2007). Lateral habenula as a source of negative reward signals in dopamine neurons. *Nature, 447*(7148): 1111–1115.

Medford, N., & Critchley, H. D. (2010). Conjoint activity of anterior insular and anterior cingulate cortex: Awareness and response. *Brain Structure and Function, 214*(5–6): 535–549.

Meerwijk, E. L., Ford, J. M., & Weiss, S. J. (2012). Brain regions associated with psychological pain: Implications for a neural network and its relationship to physical pain. *Brain Imaging and Behavior, 7*(1): 1–14.

Meier, I. M., van Honk, J., Bos, P. A., & Terburg, D. (2021). A mu-opioid feedback model of human social behavior. *Neuroscience & Biobehavioral Reviews, 121*: 250–258.

Mosri, D. F. (2021). Clinical applications of neuropsychoanalysis: Hypotheses toward an integrative model. *Frontiers in Psychology, 12*: 718372.

Mueller, S. C., Wierckx, K., & T'Sjoen, G. (2020). Neural and hormonal correlates of sexual arousal in transgender persons. *Journal of Sexual Medicine, 17*: 2495–2507.

Murphy, M. R., Checkley, S. A., Seckl, J. R., & Lightman, S. L. (1990). Naloxone inhibits oxytocin release at orgasm in man. *Journal of Clinical Endocrinology & Metabolism, 71*(4): 1056–1058.

Murphy, M. R, Seckl, J. R., Burton, S., Checkley, S. A., & Lightman, S. L. (1987). Changes in oxytocin and vasopressin secretion during sexual activity in men. *Journal of Clinical Endocrinology & Metabolism, 65*(4): 738–741.

Naruse, S. M., & Moss, M. (2019). Effects of couples' positive massage programme on wellbeing, perceived stress and coping, and relation satisfaction. *Health Psychology and Behavioral Medicine, 7*(1): 328–347.

Ophir, A. G., Wolff, J. O., & Phelps, S. M. (2008). Variation in neural V1aR predicts sexual fidelity and space use among male prairie voles in semi-natural settings. *Proceedings of the National Academy of Sciences, 105*(4): 1249–1254.

Pacey, S. (2023). *Sensate Focus and the Psyche. Integrating Sense and Sexuality in Couple Therapy*. Abingdon, UK: Routledge.

Panksepp, J. (1998). *Affective Neuroscience: The Foundations of Human and Animal Emotions*. New York: Oxford University Press.

Panksepp, J., & Biven, L. (2012). *The Archaeology of Mind*. New York: W. W. Norton.

Poeppl, T. B., Langguth, B., Rupprecht, R., Safron, A., Bzdok, D., Laird, A. R., & Eickhoff, S. B. (2016). The neural basis of sex differences in sexual behavior: A quantitative meta-analysis. *Frontiers in Neuroendocrinology, 43*: 28–43.

Poovey, K., de Jong, D. C., & Morey, K. (2022). The roles of body image, sexual motives, distraction in women's sexual pleasure. *Archives of Sexual Behavior, 51*(3): 1577–1589.

Prause, N., & Harensk, C. (2014). Inhibition, lack of excitation, or suppression: fMRI pilot of asexuality. In: K. J. Cerankowski & M. Milks (Eds.), *Asexualities: Feminist and Queer Perspectives* (pp. 35–54). New York: Taylor & Francis.

Rodríguez-Nieto, G., Sack, A. T., Dewitte, M., Emmerling, F., & Schuhmann, T. (2020). The modulatory role of cortisol in the regulation of sexual behavior in young males. *Frontiers in Behavioral Neurosciences, 14*: 552567.

Ruesink, G. B., & Georgiadis, J. R. (2017). Brain imaging of human sexual response: Recent developments and future directions. *Current Sexual Health Reports, 9*(4): 183–191.

Ruszczynski, S. P. (1992). Notes towards a psychoanalytic understanding of the couple relationship. *Psychoanalytic Psychotherapy, 6*(1): 33–48.

Schneiderman, I., Zagoory-Sharon, O., Leckman, J. F., & Feldman, R. (2012). Oxytocin during the initial stages of romantic attachment: Relations to couples' interactive reciprocity. *Psychoneuroendocrinology, 37*: 1277–1285.

Shabel, S. J., Proulx, C. D., Piriz, J., & Malinow, R. (2014). Mood regulation. GABA/glutamate co-release controls habenula output and is modified by antidepressant treatment. *Science, 345*: 1494–1498.

Siegel, D. J. (2010). *Mindsight: The New Science of Personal Transformation*. New York: Bantam.

Smith, K. S., Tindell, A. J., Aldridge, J. W., & Berridge, K. C. (2009). Ventral pallidum roles in reward and motivation. *Behavioural Brain Research, 196*(2): 155–167.

Steinglass, J. E., Berner, L. A., & Attia, E. (2019). Cognitive neuroscience of eating disorders. *Psychiatric Clinics of North America, 42*(1): 75–91.

Stoléru, S., Fonteille, V., Cornélis, C., Joyal, C., & Moulier, V. (2012). Functional neuroimaging studies of sexual arousal and orgasm in healthy men and women: A review and meta-analysis. *Neuroscience and Biobehavioral Reviews*, 36(6): 1481–1509.

Sylva, D., Safron, A., Rosenthal, A. M., Reber, P. J., Parrish, T. B., & Bailey, J. M. (2013). Neural correlates of sexual arousal in heterosexual and homosexual women and men. *Hormones and Behavior*, 64: 673–684.

Taylor, S. E. (2006). Tend and befriend. *Current Directions in Psychological Science*, 15(6): 273–277.

Thompson, A. E., Anisimowicz, Y., & Kulibert, D. (2019). A kiss is worth a thousand words: The development and validation of a scale measuring motives for romantic kissing. *Sexual and Relationship Therapy*, 34(1): 54–74.

Treas, J., & Giesen, D. (2000). Sexual infidelity among married and cohabiting Americans. *Journal of Marriage and Family*, 62(1): 48–60.

Tsapelas, I., Fisher, H. E., & Aron, A. (2010). Infidelity: when, where why. In: W. R. Cupach & B. H. Spitzberg, *The Dark Side of Close Relationships II* (pp. 175–196). New York: Routledge.

Uvnäs-Moberg, K., & Petersson, M. (2005). Oxytocin, a mediator of anti-stress, well-being, social interaction, growth and healing. *Zeitschrift für Psychosomatische Medizin und Psychotherapie*, 51(1): 57–80.

van Oort, J., Tendolkar, I., Hermans, E. J., Mulders, P. C., Beckmann, C. F., Schene, A. H., Fernández, G., & van Eijndhoven, P. F. (2017). How the brain connects in response to acute stress: A review at the human brain systems level. *Neuroscience & Biobehavioral Reviews*, 83: 281–297.

Walter, C. (2008). Affairs of the lips. *Scientific American Mind*, 19(1): 24–29.

Walum, H., Lichtenstein, P., Neiderhiser, J. M., Reiss, D., Ganiban, J. M., Spotts, E. L., Pedersen, N. L., Anckarsäter, H., Larsson, H., & Westberg, L. (2012). Variation in the oxytocin receptor gene is associated with pair-bonding and social behavior. *Biological Psychiatry*, 71(5): 419–426.

Walum, H., Westberg, L., Henningsson, S., Neiderhiser, J. M., Reiss, D., Igl, W., Ganiban, J. M., Spotts, E. L., Pedersen, N. L., Eriksson, E., & Lichtenstein, P. (2008). Genetic variation in the vasopressin receptor 1a gene (AVPR1A) associates with pair-bonding behavior in humans. *Proceedings of the National Academy of Sciences*, 105(37): 14153–14156.

Wang, W. (2018). Who cheats more? The demographics of infidelity in America. Charlottesville, VA: Institute for Family Studies.

Wazana, A. (2016). Birthweight, dopaminergic activity, and early maternal care in the prediction of disorganized attachment. *Journal of the American Academy of Child & Adolescent Psychiatry*, 55(10): S282–S283.

Wise, N. J., Frangos, E., & Komisaruk, B. R. (2017). Brain activity unique to orgasm in women: An fMRI analysis. *Journal of Sexual Medicine, 14*(11): 1380–1391.

Young, L. J., & Wang, Z. (2004). The neurobiology of pair bonding. *Nature Neuroscience, 7*(10): 1048–1054.

Zietsch, B. P., Westberg, L., Santtila, P., & Jern, P. (2015). Genetic analysis of human extrapair mating: Heritability, between-sex correlation, and receptor genes for vasopressin and oxytocin. *Evolution and Human Behavior, 36*(2): 130–136.

Index

Page numbers in **bold** indicate Glossary entries